Blue-winged Pitta

Other titles of interest:

A BIRDKEEPER'S GUIDE TO
SOFTBILLS

Bokmakierie

Photographs by Cyril Laubscher

Indian Blue-throated Flycatcher eating a mealworm

A BIRDKEEPER'S GUIDE TO

SOFTBILLS

A detailed look at this varied and colourful group of
birds, with practical advice on their care and
accommodation. Featuring a photographic survey of
more than 50 species from around the world.

David Alderton

Tetra⬤Press

No. 16082

A Salamander Book

Chestnut-flanked White-eye

Credits

Editor: Geoff Rogers   Design: Graeme Campbell
Colour reproductions:
Contemporary Lithoplates Ltd.
Filmset: SX Composing Ltd.
Printed in Portugal

Author

David Alderton has kept and bred a wide variety of birds for over twenty years. He has travelled extensively in pursuit of this interest, visiting other enthusiasts in various parts of the world, including the United States, Canada and Australia. He has previously written a number of books on avicultural subjects, and contributes regularly to general and specialist publications in the UK and overseas. David studied veterinary medicine at Cambridge University, and now, in addition to writing, runs a highly respected international service that offers advice on the needs of animals kept in both domestic and commercial environments. He is also a Council Member of the Avicultural Society.

Photographer

Cyril Laubscher has been interested in aviculture and ornithology for more than thirty years and has travelled extensively in Europe, Australia and Southern Africa photographing wildlife. When he left England for Australia in 1966 as an enthusiastic aviculturalist, this fascination found expression as he began to portray birds photographically. In Australia he met the well-known aviculturalist Stan Sindel and, as a result of this association, seventeen of Cyril's photographs were published in Joseph Forshaw's original book on Australian Parrots in 1969. Since then, his photographs have met with considerable acclaim and the majority of those that appear here were taken specially for this book.

Contents

Introduction

What are softbills? 'Softbill' is an avicultural term that covers a wide range of interesting and often colourful birds. These birds are popular with aviarists and some, notably mynahs, make excellent pets. The name 'softbill' can, however, be misleading, as none of these birds have soft beaks! In fact, the division of birds into softbill and hardbill categories is based on their dietary requirements. Whereas hardbills tend to eat seed, softbills feed on fruit, nectar, insects and other livefood. However, there can be some overlap between the two groups. Certain hardbills, such as finches, may adopt a softbill diet, particularly when breeding, while some softbills, such as Pekin Robins, will happily eat seed. Softbills are split into four groups on the basis of their feeding needs: frugivorous – fruit eating; omnivorous – most foods; insectivorous – insect eating (livefoods); nectivorous – nectar feeding. These groupings are not mutually exclusive, as the birds'

feeding habits will alter according to the time of year. Omnivorous softbills are probably the easiest group to cater for, as they will eat most foods and will readily accept inanimate foodstuffs. In contrast, it can prove difficult to persuade highly insectivorous species to accept inanimate food, and this greatly increases the risk of dietary deficiencies. Nectivorous softbills, such as hummingbirds and sunbirds, feed on nectar, but need other foods to remain healthy.

Advances in aviculture during recent years have made the care of softbills much easier. This applies particularly to feeding. Now that a wide range of prepared diets is freely available, it is not surprising that increasing numbers of softbills are being reared successfully under aviary conditions. You may be able to keep more than one species in the same cage but, generally, breeding will be more successful if the birds are housed in pairs.

Buying softbills and general care

When you are buying any kind of softbill, it is always worth travelling to see the birds before making any definite commitment. You can then inspect them closely, and get a better idea of how they have been kept and fed. Specific points need to be borne in mind for individual species, but overall, a fit softbill is alert and moves readily, especially when housed in a cage.

What to look for
Watch the birds closely before making any decisions. A bird which appears sluggish and breathes irregularly – which you can tell by looking at its tail movements – is unlikely to be healthy. The condition of the feathers, although more immediately obvious, is of rather less significance since new plumage will be grown at the next moult. The plumage of some nectivores especially can be poor if they have been kept in overcrowded conditions or have not been given adequate opportunity to bathe. A nectivore's droppings are rather sticky and will matt the feathers of any bird perching below. With care, the

Below: *A Grosbeak or Scissorbill Starling* (Scissirostrum dubium) *in fine condition. Always select birds that appear lively and alert. The condition of the feathers is less important, as the plumage will be replaced at the next moult. Before buying a bird, be sure to check the eyes, feet and vent area, as well as the general body condition.*

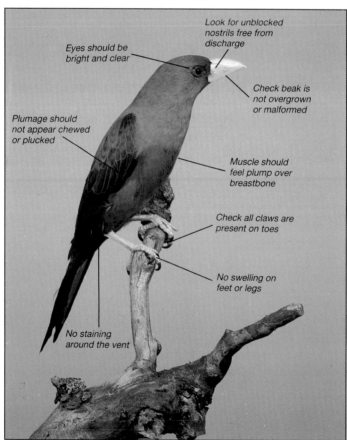

Look for unblocked nostrils free from discharge

Eyes should be bright and clear

Check beak is not overgrown or malformed

Plumage should not appear chewed or plucked

Muscle should feel plump over breastbone

Check all claws are present on toes

No swelling on feet or legs

No staining around the vent

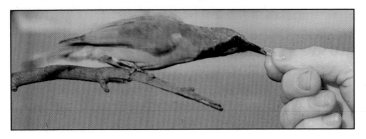

Above: *Healthy softbills have hearty appetites, but not all will be as tame as this Golden-fronted Fruitsucker. In time though, even aviary birds may feed in this way.*

birds will moult uneventfully, but will be more susceptible to chills until they have their new plumage.

Newly imported softbills are naturally more delicate than those which are well established in aviary surroundings, and will require more attention. In spite of the fact that they will have been quarantined (depending upon the country concerned), they will not be properly acclimatized, and will probably need to be kept inside over the winter. Established softbills are likely to be more expensive to buy, but are a better choice for those with little experience of bird care.

When a bird has caught your attention, look firstly at its eyes. It is not unusual for recently imported softbills to suffer from minor eye infections. These can usually be cleared up quite easily using an ophthalmic ointment or drops, although this can prove a worrying period. Look carefully at the bird's feet while it is in the cage. It should be able to grip the perch without any difficulty, its toes should be clean, and it should have a full complement of claws, particularly if you hope to exhibit the softbill.

Holding softbills
Having made a preliminary choice, ask the vendor to catch the softbills for you, so that you can examine each one at close quarters. Most softbills do not have powerful beaks, but toucans

and barbets can still inflict a painful bite on the unsuspecting handler. In any event, you should hold the majority of species with their head supported between the first and second fingers of your left hand, ensuring that the wings are held closed in your palm. You will then be able to feel the breastbone with your other hand. If you are left-handed, it may be better to reverse this so that the bird is restrained in your right hand.

The close examination
The breastbone runs down the middle of the underside of the body, starting at the lower chest. It is usually partly covered on either side by muscle tissue. If the bird is in poor condition, instead of feeling just a slight projection you will find that the sides of the breastbone are far more prominent than normal. Birds suffering from chronic ailments frequently show this sign, described as being 'light', but it is not always indicative of an infectious disease. Many softbills lose weight when adapting to an unfamiliar diet, but they should soon recover.

Check the bird's nostrils for possible blockages. A partial blockage can cause the softbill to breathe loudly, which may give a misleading impression that the bird is suffering from a more serious complaint. Blocked nostrils are not uncommon in fruit pigeons, and can be caused by a plug of food accumulating over the nostrils. If the blockage does not look too solid, rather than bathe the area, you may be able to gently prize it away from the nostrils using a blunt matchstick. Persistent nasal discharges are a much more alarming matter and will require veterinary advice. In some cases, they can be linked with eye infections.

You may want to open the bird's beak in order to check that there is no trace of mouth fungus. This is usually caused by a *Candida* infection, which is again most common in newly imported softbills. This disease is also known as thrush or candidiasis, and may result from a deficiency in Vitamin A. Nectivores are particularly at risk, especially if their nectar contains a high level of sugar, which appears to encourage candidiasis.

It may not even be necessary to open the bird's beak to recognize this affliction. A hummingbird perching with its tongue protruding outside its beak is liable to be infected. This bird will endanger the others sharing its quarters and should therefore be isolated. It is very important that you disinfect the drinkers, because it is through them that the infection is usually spread. Treatment will often be effective in mild cases, but there is always a risk that the whitish growths of *Candida* will spread down the digestive tract into the crop and beyond, where medication is unlikely to be successful.

Parasites can affect all softbills, although they are not always easy to detect during a casual examination. Nevertheless, open the wings and look for any signs of lice. These external parasites have a fairly elongated shape and are generally visible to the naked eye, in contrast to mites. Treatment for all ectoparasites (i.e. those occurring on the surface of the body) is straightforward, and should be carried out routinely on all newly acquired birds.

Internal parasites can be considerably harder to recognize without laboratory tests, and they may contribute to weight loss. Parasites within the digestive tract may cause loose droppings, which you should be able to see on the floor of the cage. Certainly, if the plumage around the vent is soiled, the bird is likely to have suffered a digestive disturbance, which could be either parasitic or infectious in origin. Think very carefully before acquiring a bird in this state, and keep it in strict isolation until an accurate diagnosis can be made.

The feet
Holding the softbill in your hand, carry out a detailed examination of its feet, especially the undersurfaces since these are not visible when it is perching. Look for any evidence of swelling or soreness, which could be indicative of bumblefoot. Ideally, the claws should all be well formed and not misshapen, but you can trim these back later if necessary.

Below: *You can apply a split plastic ring or band like this to a bird of any age. They are useful for identifying individual birds.*

Below: *This Grey Go-away Bird has one claw missing. Be sure to check the feet and claws for any malformation before buying.*

Above: *Softbills housed in an aviary can become surprisingly tame. This is a Grey Go-away Bird, a member of the Touraco family.*

However, an accumulation of faecal matter on the foot will require immediate action. If dirt is allowed to dry on the digits, it can restrict the circulation and may cause the loss of a toe as a result of dry gangrene. This is particularly likely if the whole of the toe is encased in faecal matter.

Do not attempt to break off the debris, since you may remove the claw or even part of the digit in the process. Instead, fill a clean disposable container, such as a yoghurt pot, with tepid water and immerse the bird's whole foot in the water; keep it submerged for several minutes. Then, very carefully using a finger nail, chip off the accumulated material, starting with the claw and moving up the toe. Do this without rushing, softening the dirt by immersing the foot in water again if necessary. Rinse the foot in clean, cold water, which will help to quell any minor bleeding. Finally, smear an antiseptic cream over the toes, rubbing the medication in carefully so that it will not be wiped off on a perch once you let the bird loose. Obviously, the softbill's environmental conditions should

be improved to prevent this happening again.

In the case of nectivores, and hummingbirds especially, look for any signs of swelling close to the joints. Although this could be bumblefoot, it is probably more likely to be gout, and you may be able to feel the firm deposits of urates (crystals of uric acid salts) beneath the skin. This contrasts with the fairly fluid swelling caused by bumblefoot. There is no direct treatment for gout in birds, and the human drugs tend to be toxic for them. Ultimately, affected birds are likely to lose the outside toe, as the blood supply to the digit is restricted. Although this need not handicap them unduly, other less evident but more serious symptoms may be affecting the body organs. It is best, therefore, not to buy a bird if you suspect that it is suffering from gout.

Travelling home
Ensure that your softbills are properly boxed so that they cannot escape on the journey home. For bigger birds, wooden containers with secure lids are best, and it is safer to transport toucans and hornbills in individual boxes, because of their prominent beaks. Put some fruit in the boxes for the birds to eat during the journey.

Nectivores, too, should be

Above: *This Black-eared Golden Tanager, like all softbills, needs to bathe to maintain its plumage. A light spray may also be useful.*

boxed separately because, in spite of their relatively small size, these birds can be aggressive towards each other. Since hummingbirds, especially, need to feed almost constantly during the hours of daylight, you should include a feeder in their transport box. As these birds must be kept in the light, their boxes are usually made of corrugated plastic. Fix a partially filled nectar feeder on to the outside of the box, with the tube projecting inside. Then fit a low perch inside the box. Always check that the box has adequate ventilation in the form of airholes, ideally in both the sides and top, so that warm air can escape.

Initial care

On arrival, prepare the birds' food and place it in their quarters before you release them. If you have bought more than one bird, it is best to house them separately to allow them to recover from the journey.

Although the birds' quarters may be heated at first, you should aim to reduce the temperature gradually, especially if they are to be transferred to an outdoor aviary. In temperate climates, you will have to wait until the late spring to move them, to avoid any risk of snow or frost.

It can be difficult to introduce a newcomer to quarters occupied by an established bird, even if they are of the opposite sex. Therefore, to minimize the likelihood of the new bird being harassed, move the present occupant to separate quarters several days beforehand. You will then be able to release both birds into the aviary simultaneously, having removed the territorial advantage of the established individual. Be sure to provide an adequate choice of feeding dishes, especially at first, so that the birds can both have ready access to food without coming into conflict with each other. You may want to confine them within the shelter to begin with, as this is where they will normally be fed.

Plastic food containers that hook on to the aviary netting are popular with softbill keepers. They are durable, easy to clean, and can be positioned anywhere in the aviary. Water is usually provided in a drinker rather than in an open container, so that it does not become contaminated. All birds should be offered fresh drinking water every day. This includes nectivores, although they may not actually drink very much.

Floor feeding is favoured by some softbill enthusiasts, but in an aviary this should only be done in the shelter, where the floor is adequately lined with newspaper. Change the newspaper each day when the food pot is removed. In this way the softfood will not be spattered on to the aviary netting, which can be difficult to clean. Heavy ceramic containers, frequently sold as dogs' water bowls, are ideal for this purpose since they can be cleaned easily and thoroughly.

Bathing
A ceramic dogs' bowl filled with water can also be used as a bird bath. Many species bathe readily, but make sure that the bird's plumage is still watertight before you allow it to get wet. The secretions which help to prevent the bird becoming waterlogged in the rain are produced from the preen gland just above the tail. When birds are kept indoors for any length of time, the waterproofing effect of the

Below: *A range of outside flights. It may not be possible to transfer new arrivals immediately to outside accommodation; a period of acclimatization is often necessary.*

secretion is lost, and the plumage tends to become dry and brittle. If it uses a bath or sits outside in a shower of rain, the bird will become soaked to its skin, and is then more likely to become chilled. It will not be able to fly until its plumage dries out completely, and it may even drown in a shallow container of water.

Therefore, do not offer a bath to a newly acquired softbill which has been kept indoors. Instead, gently spray the bird with water each day, using a plant sprayer. This will encourage the bird to preen itself and the waterproofing of the feathers will soon be restored. The oil from the preen gland gives a shiny gloss to the plumage, compared with the dull, rather scruffy appearance of a bird which has not had the opportunity to bathe regularly.

The bathing habits of softbills do differ quite noticeably, however. While some birds, such as tanagers, will immerse themselves readily in a container of water, others, such as fruit pigeons, will only bathe in a shower of rain. It is possible to obtain plumage conditioners which you can add to the water for spraying softbills housed indoors. This can be helpful, but it is not a substitute for allowing the birds to bathe regularly out of doors.

If you provide the birds with an open container of water for bathing purposes, do not leave this in the birds' quarters for any length of time. Once it has been used by the birds, the water will be soiled and unfit for drinking. Therefore, it is a good idea to provide the bath a couple of hours before you clean out the birds' quarters. Another reason is that the birds will splash water onto the newspaper, which you can then change.

The acclimatization period
Do not be in too much of a hurry to move the softbills outside into the aviary. The ideal time to acquire recently imported birds is in the early summer because, once they have settled in, you can quickly

release them into the aviary. However, this can be a difficult period if other birds are already established in the aviary, because they are liable to be approaching breeding condition and may already have started nesting activities. The introduction of newcomers at this stage is likely to upset the balance within a mixed aviary, and may cause breeding birds to desert their nests.

Problems with the new birds are most likely to become apparent soon after they have been moved to the aviary. Check that they are eating adequately in their new surroundings and encourage them to roost in the shelter, as suggested previously. The more insectivorous softbills can be difficult to wean off a diet consisting mainly of livefood. If possible, do this before moving them to the aviary.

There are various techniques for 'meating off', as this manipulation of the diet is sometimes called. The most straightforward method, using mealworms, involves mixing the larvae very thoroughly with inanimate food. When the bird picks the mealworms out of the food pot, it will also be getting some of the feeding mixture which will have stuck to them, and soon it should start to eat this food willingly. The timescale is somewhat variable, but most softbills should be feeding quite readily on other foods within a fortnight or so. In most cases, this task will have been undertaken during the quarantine period, but some individuals can prove harder to meat off than others, and the process may not be finished by the end of this time.

Moulting
Most birds shed their feathers annually and this can be a debilitating period for them. It is important, therefore, to keep a careful watch on softbills at this time for any signs of illness. A varied diet will certainly help to speed the birds through this phase. You may also want to use a

food supplement, especially when the birds are actually moulting. Various brands are available, and although those containing vitamins and minerals are useful, the ones with a wider range of ingredients including the essential amino-acids – are preferable. It is easy to give softbills these powdered preparations, either by mixing them with mealworms for the insectivorous species, or sprinkling them over fruit in the food bowl. If the birds eat a varied diet, they are less likely to be deficient, but supplements can be very important particularly for newly acquired insectivores.

Daily care
Keeping softbills can be a demanding hobby, since the birds will need attention every day. It is usual to check the stock in the morning and also provide fresh food at this time. You must wash

Below: A cock Amethyst Starling moulting; new feathers emerge through existing plumage. A varied diet plus food supplements are vital at this difficult time.

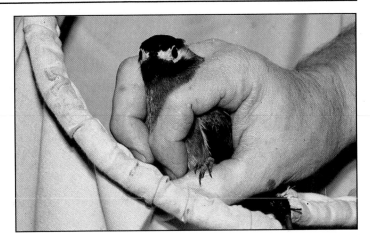

all feeding containers thoroughly with a detergent, and then rinse them well before refilling them. It may be easier to alternate two sets of feeding dishes, especially if you do not have much time in the morning. You can then leave the pots immersed in a disinfectant solution during the day and wash them at night, ready for use the next day.

Keep water pots clean, using a bottle brush for tubular drinkers. If water containers are left in the sun, this will inevitably result in algal growth, which may prove harmful as some algae produce toxins. Wash out water containers once a week, and after using them for tonics and medication of any kind.

Even on a busy day, take time to look at the birds so that you can spot any signs of illness at an early stage, thus greatly increasing the likelihood of successful treatment. The temperaments of the softbills in a mixed aviary will almost certainly change through the year. Watching their behaviour will enable you to recognize whether a bird is being bullied. You can then remove the bird from the aviary before any real harm is done.

Catching softbills
There are various ways of catching softbills, and the method used depends to some extent on the species concerned. A fairly deep net, well padded around the rim, is

Above: *A White-eared Sibia* (Heterophasia auricularis) *being carefully removed from a catching net. The toes may need to be freed individually from the material.*

useful for catching many species, including most of the smaller softbills. You may prefer to catch bigger birds, such as mynahs, with your hands. It is wise to wear a pair of thin gloves for protection, particularly if you are handling birds, such as toucans, which can inflict quite a painful bite.

In order to minimize the stress for the birds, try to catch them with as little disturbance as possible. Remove all perches before you start, so that the birds either cling to the aviary netting, or fly down on to the floor, where they can be restrained quite easily. When the bird is on the wire mesh or in the net, it will tighten its grip as soon as it is touched. Remove its claws very gently from the netting, holding it in your other hand so that it does not escape.

Catching a bird in an aviary can prove an unnerving experience at first, and certain species require special care. Toucans can injure their long beaks since these are not in fact solid but have a honeycombed structure. Fruit pigeons, like touracos, have very loose plumage, which they shed very easily when caught. This can be disconcerting, but is not a

19

cause for concern. Both groups are rather nervous when approached at close quarters, and tend to fly vertically if they feel threatened. As this can result in a head injury, encourage them to fly down to the aviary floor by reaching above them. Never approach the birds from below perch level, as this is likely to panic them and make them fly upwards.

Hummingbirds and other small nectivores can be particularly difficult to catch because of their agility in flight. If you encounter problems, do not continue your attempts if the bird appears stressed and is breathing very heavily, since this can prove fatal. As an alternative, you can use a cage trap. All you need for this is an empty cage. Put it in the aviary and remove all food containers. Place a drinker in the cage, keeping the door open by pulling on a piece of string. Once the bird enters the cage, you should be able to close the door by releasing the string. The bird will then be trapped inside. This method, although sometimes time consuming, is much less distressing for the bird.

The easiest time to catch a hummingbird in an aviary is after dark. At this time, the birds will be torpid, resting on a perch conserving their body heat. However, this method is not recommended if there are other species in the immediate vicinity. Unlike the hummingbird, they are likely to be frightened by your presence and may start flying madly around the aviary, possibly injuring themselves as a result.

Mice and rats
Night fright is commonly associated with the presence of rodents in the aviary. Mice are a particular problem because they can squeeze through a small gap, although 1.25cm (0.5in) square aviary mesh should exclude them quite effectively. You may not actually see the mice, but their droppings in, or close to, food pots are unmistakable. They will almost

certainly disturb breeding birds, although some larger softbills, such as toucans and mynahs, may in fact catch mice. Do not encourage this however, but take immediate steps to eliminate the rodents, because they represent a major health threat to the birds. Various diseases to which softbills are susceptible, such as pseudotuberculosis, can be introduced to an aviary by rodents.

In a birdroom with an electrical supply, you can use an ultrasonic rodent deterrent. This operates by emitting high-pitched sound waves that affect the rodents' nervous system, making them feel uncomfortable. It has no adverse effects on the birds, however.

Unfortunately, this system is of no value in an outside flight, which is the part of the aviary where the rodents may be coming in. All you can do here is try to block their access routes and encourage them to feed in a live trap. This is basically an open box, which the mice will enter readily to get to the food. After several nights, when the mice are used to the box, fit a top unit with metal gauze tunnels. The mice will go through the tunnels to reach the food, but they will be unable to escape.

A similar system is available for rats, which are more likely to attack the birds, and even eat them in some cases. However, if you suspect the presence of rats, it may be best to call in a professional pest control firm, who will undertake their elimination with minimum delay.

Cats
Cats can also be a problem, although they may of course catch mice around the aviary. Your own cat will probably ignore the birds once it is used to their presence, but neighbouring cats are likely to be more curious. They may take to climbing on to the aviary, frightening the occupants.

The best way to prevent them from doing this is to construct a barrier around the top of the aviary, using strands of wire. Fix these on to vertical pieces of timber as if you are making a fence. Since the cats will be unable to climb over this, they should stop trying to reach the birds from above. The birds will not be so distressed if the cats are on the ground. A well-aimed water pistol can then be used to deter any persistent ones from hanging around the aviary.

Wintertime care
Birds which are to live outside throughout the year will need to be fully acclimatized. If they are imported, they will probably have to spend their first winter in heated accommodation indoors, before being released back into the aviary in the spring. You must ensure that the birds are adequately protected when the weather is bad. On a cold day the wind can reduce the temperature still further, so shield the birds from its effects, using plastic frames around the sides of the aviary (see page 32).

Leave part of the roof uncovered, however, as this will provide ventilation. In addition, if it snows, there is a danger that the weight of snow on plastic sheeting covering the wire mesh may cause this to bow badly. In extreme circumstances, it might even collapse. This is less likely to

Below: *Some softbills can be kept outside throughout the year, once they are fully acclimatized. Take extra care during bad weather.*

happen to the shelter roof, since here the sheeting is sloped, and not fixed directly on to the frame.

Try to ensure that perches remain free of snow. However, the greatest risk period for frostbite tends to be when a thaw has set in. The perches then become wet and this moisture freezes during the night. A perch heater is therefore extremely useful to protect birds that insist on roosting in the flight. (See page 37 for more information on perch heaters.)

In severe weather, the bird's food is liable to freeze, so check on this two or three times a day. It is wise to make some alterations to the diet at this time of year, taking account of the birds' increased energy expenditure. You can offer soaked sultanas, which have a higher food value than fresh fruit, a little cheese cut into small pieces and even diced boiled potatoes. Do not worry about cutting the potatoes into very small pieces, as they will break up easily when they are cooked. Potatoes are valuable for certain thrushes, but they may not be popular with all softbills.

Also ensure that the birds have a constant supply of water, but deter them from bathing in sub-zero temperatures. Do not completely fill the water containers because they are liable to crack with the expansion of the water as it freezes. You can add a small amount of glycerine to the water to prevent it from freezing too quickly, but it is preferable simply to change the water as necessary during the day. To do this, immerse the drinker in a bowl of warm, but not boiling, water and soon the ice plug will float out, allowing you to refill the container.

Provided that softbills are adequately acclimatized and have ready access to both food and water, they will be able to survive a spell of cold weather without any problem. In fact, although softbills are popularly thought to be rather exotic and delicate birds, many are accustomed to cold weather in their homelands, particularly those species that live at high altitudes.

21

Housing

Housing softbills is a complex matter, depending on various considerations, notably which species you want to keep and the area where you live. For a start, you will need a flight cage. This will enable you to check that the birds are healthy before releasing them into the aviary. Flight cages can also be useful for overwintering stock indoors. However, since softbills are generally very active, and because they also require retreats within their quarters, this form of housing is certainly not recommended for use on a permanent basis for most species.

The box type of cage is favoured for all softbills, since it prevents food and droppings falling outside the cage. This design also provides the birds with a greater sense of security than an open wire cage since all the sides, apart from the front, are enclosed.

Mynah cages

Unfortunately, most pet mynah birds are kept in highly unsuitable cages. If you are going to keep one of these birds, do not be persuaded to buy one of the small, box-type cages which are usually sold for mynahs. Ask if the shop can obtain a larger flight cage for you. There are now some attractive designs on the market, although you are only likely to see them in larger pet stores with the space to display them. Check that the cage can be cleaned thoroughly and easily, since mynah birds are messy and their quarters will need daily attention as a result.

Building a flight cage

If you are unable to purchase a suitable cage for your bird, you can make one without too much difficulty.

Since cleanliness is a vital consideration, it is probably best to avoid plywood because food and droppings tend to stick to it. These can be difficult to remove and, in outdoor surroundings especially, may turn mouldy. Neither is hardboard a suitable material. Although easier to clean than plywood, it weakens and warps if it becomes saturated with water. This could be a problem with mynah birds and many other softbills which, if given the chance, will bathe daily, soaking their quarters in the process.

Not surprisingly, therefore, these traditional materials have become less popular since the advent of melamine-covered chipboard. This material can be easily wiped clean with a damp cloth and does not become unsightly with age. It is versatile and can be cut as required. However, since several sheets will result in a fairly heavy structure, you may want to construct a secure base fitted with castors for the cage.

The size of the flight cage depends to some extent on the species you intend to keep. A mynah bird should be housed in a flight about 180x90x90cm (6x3x3ft). Only in accommodation of this size will you be able to enjoy to the full the lively personality of your pet. Obesity can be a problem in softbills, especially in gross feeders like mynahs, and it will certainly shorten their lifespan. The combination of cramped quarters and the warm environment of most homes puts many pet mynahs at risk from the effects of obesity, since they use little energy and enjoy free access to food.

The front of the cage will be the hardest part to construct. Make a separate wooden framework using 2.5cm (1in) square timber. You may want to paint this, either to match the colour of the sides or to create a contrast. Remember that the interior should be light, so that the birds are seen to best effect.

Access to the cage

A removable floor tray will facilitate cleaning, so leave a gap for this at the bottom of the front section. To do this, simply make the front framework about 2.5cm (1in) shorter than the other sides, so that there is a space at the base of the cage. The tray can be made of plywood or it can match the framework of the front unit. A handle in the centre will allow you to pull it out easily. Sides around the tray will contain the dirt, but since these tend to become soiled, a flat sheet of plywood fixed to the front piece, creating a drawer-like appearance, is preferable.

In most cases access to the cage will be via a door in the front unit. The size of the door is an important consideration, since if it is too large, the birds are liable to escape every time it is opened. As a general guide, make it just large enough for your hand to fit through easily. There should then be little space for the birds to slip past you when you open the door. Position the door relatively low down, close to the bottom of the frame. The birds will then feel less threatened and are more likely to remain on their perches, rather than attempt to escape through the opening. Incorporate the framework for the door into the front section before this is wired over. The door should be hinged to open outwards rather than inwards. A small clasp fitted opposite the hinges will ensure that it can be securely closed.

Wire mesh

It is now possible to obtain wire mesh coated with green PVC. This is ideal for use with most softbills, since it can be wiped clean and washed without fear of the wire beneath rusting as a result of the exposure to water. Avoid buying any mesh that is damaged. Apart from looking unattractive, it will rust. You can still use ordinary galvanized mesh, but this tends to look rather harsh in comparison with the PVC-covered mesh, and this in turn will clearly affect the appearance of the birds.

The actual size of the mesh you choose will depend on the species you are keeping. For small

Flight cage suitable for mynah bird

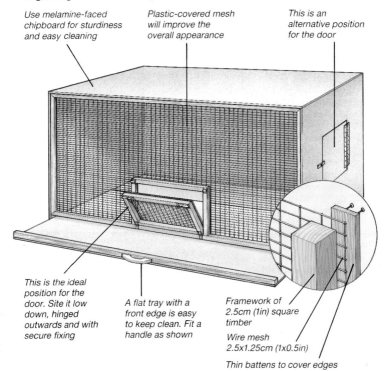

Use melamine-faced chipboard for sturdiness and easy cleaning

Plastic-covered mesh will improve the overall appearance

This is an alternative position for the door

This is the ideal position for the door. Site it low down, hinged outwards and with secure fixing

A flat tray with a front edge is easy to keep clean. Fit a handle as shown

Framework of 2.5cm (1in) square timber

Wire mesh 2.5x1.25cm (1x0.5in)

Thin battens to cover edges

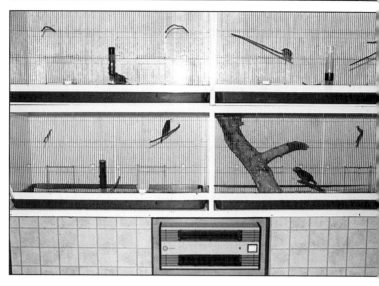

softbills, it is best to use netting which is 1.25cm (0.5in) square. Large birds, such as mynahs, will need a 2.5x1.25cm (1x 0.5in) mesh. The size of the mesh is especially important in outside flights, and you may therefore prefer to buy mesh that is suitable for both indoor and outdoor use, if you want to keep the birds in an aviary for part of the year.

If the frame is 180cm (6ft) in length, you will have to run the mesh horizontally, because most mesh is only 90cm (3ft) wide. Alternatively, you can fix it vertically with a central divider in the framework. However, this can look rather unsightly, particularly as rectangular mesh is less attractive if the rectangles run vertically. Certainly, for a cage in the home, square mesh is more versatile, albeit more expensive.

Tack the top corners of the mesh in place using netting staples. Unroll the wire, keeping it both taut and level, using the sides of the frame as a guide. Hold the bottom edge of the mesh in place, check the positioning, then tack it in place with netting staples. Using wire cutters, free the roll and then cut a hole where the door is to go. Try to cut as close as possible to the strand above, so that the sharp

Above: *A typical set of cages in an indoor birdroom. These can be useful for either acclimatizing or overwintering birds. The heater and thermostat are at bottom.*

Below: *Check that perches in the cage or aviary are of a suitable size. Clean or replace them regularly to avoid foot disorders.*

edges are kept to a minimum. Fix the mesh firmly around the door frame in the same way as for the main framework.

Any protruding edges of mesh will obviously be dangerous to the birds. You should therefore tack thin (2.5cm/1in) battening all around the edge of the frame, using panel pins. This will cover the exposed wire ends. Battening should also be fitted around both the door and the door frame.

Perches

It will probably be easier to put the perches in from above. Therefore, when you assemble the flight cage, fit the roof on last. Again, the choice of perches will depend to a great extent on the birds you are keeping. The thickness of the perches should enable the birds to exercise their toes, and some variation is therefore desirable, but this should not be excessive. If the perches are too thin, the front claws may actually curl round and penetrate the sole of the foot, as the bird struggles to retain its balance. When bacteria enters the wound, the result is a localized swelling, popularly known as 'bumblefoot' (see also page 15).

Softbills in cages are particularly at risk from this affliction because when they hop about on the floor, they step in their droppings. The faecal matter sticks to their feet and contaminate the perches. Any damage to the skin on the underside of the foot, even if it is not caused by the claws, may result in an infection.

Hard perches can have a similar effect, since the bird has to retain a constant grip, applying pressure to the same parts of the foot. These in turn will become inflamed and abrasions may then occur. Dowelling is therefore unsuitable for perches. Try to obtain natural branches, which can be cut to the appropriate length.

For mynah birds, you will need two relatively straight perches, but for the lively smaller softbills, a main branch with several side-shoots is recommended. This allows the birds to dart up and down the branches as they would in the wild. Fruit trees are a traditional source of perches, but it is best to avoid any which may have been recently sprayed with chemicals. The bird may hold food against the perch and there is a risk of contamination. In any event, wash the branches before using them as they may have been soiled by wild birds whose droppings could prove harmful to the softbills.

Perches in the flight cage should be firmly fixed in position, but in such a way that they can be easily removed with the minimum of disturbance. Branches, particularly for the small nectivores, should be replaced regularly as they dry out and lose their suppleness, leaving the birds at risk from sore feet. Similarly, as they become soiled, the perches will have to be either scrubbed clean or discarded.

Take particular care not to distort the netting when fixing perches at the front of the flight cage. Over a period of time, particularly with heavy birds such as mynahs, the movement back and forth along the perches may weaken the mesh enough to cause holes. It is often better, therefore, to fix the perches to the door frame in order to provide stability without damaging the mesh. Perches are invariably positioned across the cage rather than lengthways so that the birds have more flying space. Make sure, however, that your softbills can turn around easily at both ends of the perches without damaging their tails.

Flooring

The usual floor covering is several sheets of newspaper. This is freely available and very absorbent. Although not attractive, it can be changed easily and is not messy, unlike other floor-coverings such as sawdust, shredded paper and shavings. Stick adjoining sheets of newspaper together with clear tape, as the draught caused when the birds fly may blow them apart.

Most of the droppings will collect under the perches, and you should put a thicker layer of newspaper here. Avoid bird sand because of its abrasive nature, which could damage the feet of softbills if they spend a great deal of time on the floor. Furthermore, it sticks readily to fruit and other moist food and may be eaten accidentally.

Potential problems
While most softbills will not damage their surroundings, some can be destructive to woodwork. Woodpeckers, not surprisingly, can do a great deal of damage in a relatively short space of time, but they are not often kept in captivity. Toucans and certain barbets, however, can use their beaks in a similar effective manner. When you design a flight cage for these birds, therefore, include additional battening or a wire mesh framework to protect the wood.

Make this protective framework with 3.75cm (1.5in) timber. Cover the whole face of the frame with the mesh and batten the cut edges top and bottom. Alternatively, extend the mesh for a short distance, so that it can be bent over and fixed to the top and bottom sides of the frame. Then, when the roof is fitted, the sharp edges of the mesh will be inaccessible to the birds, and all the woodwork, apart from the perches, will be protected.

The destructive capabilities of these softbills vary somewhat, with some individuals being worse offenders than others. In newly-acquired stock, such traits are less likely to be seen, since they are often linked to the onset of the breeding period. The birds attack the aviary woodwork as a substitute for building a nesting site and providing a suitable nestbox will often modify their behaviour.

In order to prevent droppings and food falling outside the flight cage, you can screen the sides with rigid plastic sheeting. But do not extend this right down to ground level. Leave the bottom open so that any debris which drops down through the mesh can be easily cleaned up.

The outdoor aviary
The outside flight section of an aviary is built in a similar way to a cage. In this instance, however, the timber should be treated to prevent it rotting. It is now possible to obtain lengths of timber which have been impregnated with a suitable chemical. This will save a great deal of time as you can start to make the frames immediately, rather than apply several coats of a suitable treatment and then wait for the timber to dry out.

Instead of simply nailing the lengths of timber together, it is better to cut joints and assemble the frames with screws. The standard half-lap joint will serve well for this purpose, helping to strengthen the overall structure. Build the panels to fit the width of the netting you intend to use as this will save time and expense. Making the frames up individually gives you a sectional structure which can later be moved or expanded quite easily.

The overall dimensions of the flight will again depend on the species. Larger softbills, such as the touracos, need correspondingly bigger flights. During the breeding season, cock birds can prove quite aggressive towards their mate. In cramped surroundings the situation will be aggravated since the hen will have less space to retreat from her over-ardent mate.

Another point to consider is the likely number of birds to be housed together. Generally, the flight should not be less than 2.7m (9ft) long, and it may need to be double this length for birds such as touracos. The aviary should be high enough to allow you to stand without difficulty, and at least 90cm (3ft) wide.

Access to the aviary
The next point to consider is where to locate the doors. The flight is

connected to an enclosed area behind – known as the shelter – which may look like a small shed. Alternatively, it can be simply a raised area, either built into the flight or standing on legs outside it. Clearly, this is the cheaper option, but it will be less versatile. In this case, access is likely to be via the flight, which can be disturbing to the birds, especially during the breeding period.

There is always a connecting door between the shelter and flight, but it is a good idea to include a separate means of entry to both parts of the aviary, if possible. The birds will invariably be fed in the shelter, but are likely to nest in the flight. Therefore, if you only have space for one outside door, it is best if this opens into the shelter. You can then enter the flight through the connecting door, thus causing much less disturbance to the birds than if you walked through the flight to reach the shelter.

The safety porch
There is always a risk that a bird may escape when the aviary door is opened, so you should incorporate a safety porch into the aviary design. While some birds may remain close to the aviary or return to it if they escape, it is much more likely that they will be lost. A safety porch provides a double-door entry system, which ensures that even if a bird does slip out through the aviary door, it will remain within the porch.

The safety porch need not be a large structure: 90x90cm (3x3ft) is adequate. Build the framework in the same way as for the aviary flight, and cover it with mesh. The arrangement of the two doors is important. If the outer door opens inwards, this will occupy space, restricting entry to and from the aviary. Ensure, therefore, that the door leading into the safety porch opens outwards, and that the aviary door is hinged in the opposite direction.

The shelter
The primary function of the shelter is to provide the birds with a dry area where they can roost at night and during bad weather. A basic shed-like structure will therefore suffice in most cases. The dimensions of the shelter will again

Below: *One of the great pleasures on a summer's day is to sit quietly by the aviary and watch the birds in the flight, especially if they have chicks. They will soon accept your presence without showing any signs of fear. When planning the aviary, try to site it so that you can enjoy it to its best advantage.*

depend on the species of softbills being kept, but a typical size would be 90x90cm (3x3ft).

Build a basic framework, as constructed for the flight. Tongued and grooved timber is recommended for cladding the sides, so that the interior will be quite draught-proof. It is important to include a window in the shelter, because the birds will be reluctant to enter if the interior is dark. Make allowance for this when constructing the framework by providing extra supports in the frame. Another window can also be incorporated into the door at the back of the shelter. This will improve the lighting without having a large expanse of glass which could act as a heat trap.

It is better to use frosted glass in order to give the birds a greater sense of security. You may want to fit double-glazed panels which will improve the insulation of the structure. This is especially important if the softbills are to be kept outside without heat throughout the year.

As you make up the frames, mark them so that you know where each one fits. The connecting frame, linking the flight and aviary, will require a landing platform and access hole for the birds. The platform can be a simple flat piece of wood and should extend into the shelter from the flight. It is

usual to cut the access hole about 150cm (5ft) from the ground in order to incorporate the platform. The actual size of the platform and dimensions of the hole again depend to a certain extent on the birds you are keeping.

A relatively small access hole is recommended, in order to minimize heat loss from the shelter. However, the birds will be reluctant to use it if it is too small, as they will feel trapped in the shelter if they cannot get out easily. As an added refinement, the run of the landing platform can be edged, giving it a tray-like appearance. This offers the birds more security, and will also help protect them from the wind when they are in the shelter.

If you adapt a small shed to form the shelter, this will save you worrying about building the roof. If you are making your own shelter, it is better not to have an apex roof as this can appear rather unsightly and is not as easy to construct as a flat roof. A flat roof should be slightly sloped, so that rainwater will drain off rapidly. It is usual to

Below: *Plants are an important feature of any softbill aviary. Apart from providing cover, they also attract insects, which the birds consume avidly, especially when breeding. Annuals planted in the spring will grow quickly.*

slope the roof so that the lowest point is at the back of the shelter.

The roof section should be slightly larger than the outer dimensions of the shelter. Once the shelter has been erected, it will in fact slot over the side panels and can be fixed firmly in place. Heavy duty plywood is often used for cladding the roof. This material is quite robust, and roofing felt can be easily and securely attached to it by means of felt nails.

Ready-built aviaries

Instead of building your own aviary, you can of course purchase one of the designs made by specialist firms, who often advertise in avicultural journals. In addition to complete packages, you can also buy individual units which allow you to plan your own aviary. Try to visit the supplier before purchasing an aviary since, even a small unit will be a costly investment and price is not always a reflection of quality. Points to check include whether the panels are properly jointed, rather than being simply nailed together, and whether the timber has been treated with a wood preservative. It is of course possible to have an aviary built entirely to your own specifications, but this will be considerably more expensive.

Apart from the traditional rectangular structure, you may be attracted towards a multi-sided aviary, such as an octagonal design, with a central shelter. Although these may look more appealing, they tend not to be very satisfactory. The birds are more likely to be disturbed when you attend to them in a multi-sided aviary, because you cannot avoid entering through the flight. Moreover, accommodation of this type is much more exposed to the elements unless you cover some of the sides with plastic sheeting. Flying space is vital for many softbills but, unless an aviary of this design is very large, there will be only a relatively small area available, causing the birds to fly around in a circle.

Siting the aviary

It is obviously best to choose a relatively sheltered spot for the aviary, taking advantage of any particular garden feature, such as a bank or hedge, which will provide natural protection from the elements. Try to make the aviary blend in with the garden so that, in time, it will become an attractive feature. The surroundings should be well lit and not excessively shaded by trees. A location where the birds are visible from the house is best, but check before making any final decision that you are not infringing any planning restrictions.

Constructing the aviary

It is also helpful to locate the aviary close to the house for construction purposes, so that you can have ready access to power and water supplies. The first step is to prepare the site, bearing in mind that the surrounding garden will inevitably be damaged. You should therefore move any valuable plants and cut the lawn into turves, before you start work. You may want to replant the grass, so transfer the turves to an area of shady open ground. Keep them well watered so that the roots do not dry out.

The best time to construct an aviary is in the early spring. Many people like to include plants in the flight, and planting at this time of year allows the vegetation to establish itself. Similarly, the birds will have ample time to settle into their quarters before winter.

Having cleared the site, ensure that it is level. The next step is to construct the footings on which the aviary will rest. A secure base is important, for structural reasons and also to keep out vermin, which will tunnel under inadequate foundations and get into the aviary. Carefully mark out the dimensions of the structure, remembering to include the safety porch and shelter. Dig trenches around the perimeter, making them about 45cm (18in) deep. Then lay a bed of concrete in the bottom of the trench and put in blocks.

A typical softbill aviary

Inner (solid) door leading to birdroom/shelter

Stock or flight cages

Inner wire mesh door leading into shelter

Brick or block foundations prevent rot of aviary woodwork

Wire mesh door into flight

Shrub provides nesting cover

Door of safety porch opens outwards

Below: *The simplest aviary plan, suitable for hardy softbills.*

Below: *A plan view of the aviary shown in the illustration above.*

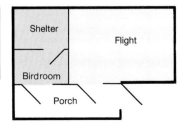

Shelter	Flight
Porch	

Shelter	Flight
Birdroom	
Porch	

Entrance for birds into shelter, shielded to lessen draughts

Corrugated plastic sheeting on part of roof provides weather protection

Foundations extend below ground

Tree branch set firmly in pot

Left: *A plan of a typical softbill aviary. A safety porch is essential to prevent the birds escaping when you enter the aviary. The entrance hole gives the birds easy access to the shelter. Position the perches here at a higher level than in the flight to encourage the birds to roost inside. Ensure that perches are accessible so that you can clean and replace them regularly. There are, of course, alternative designs of aviary, but all are constructed on similar lines.*

At this stage it is worth widening the trench in order to pack hardcore in behind the blocks once the mortar has dried. This will provide some drainage. Above ground level, you may prefer to use bricks rather than blocks, but you must ensure that they are level, with successive layers overlapping correctly. Continue the brickwork to a height of at least 30cm(1ft) above ground level, to prevent the aviary wood rotting through contact with the soil and absorbing moisture.

Leave the base to dry thoroughly. You can now start to assemble the frames of the aviary but, certainly by this stage, you will need assistance. Frame-fixers, which fit through the timber into the brickwork below, offer a simple means of attaching the sections to the footings.

Join one end panel to a side one, creating a right-angle. You can also use frame-fixers for the panels, or you can bolt them together instead. The advantage of a sectional aviary is that you will be able to dismantle it later, saving considerable expense if you move home. Make sure the bolts are well oiled and equipped with washers as well as nuts.

Do not attempt to hang the doors until the whole aviary has been assembled. In any event, they would be in the way while you are finishing off the interior of the structure. Remember to batten over any loose ends of netting. Once the aviary is structurally sound, you can attend to the

Below: *Here, the porch offers combined access to all shelters.*

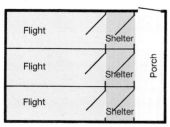

roofing. Translucent plastic sheeting, which will give protection against the elements, is ideal for the roof of the flight. It is best to buy flat sheets, preferably treated against ultraviolet light in order to prolong their lifespan.

Depending on the size of the flight and local climatic conditions, the plastic should cover at least 120cm (4ft) of the flight and should slope downwards, away from the shelter. Particularly if you have a planted flight, you will need to fit guttering along the lower edge of the roof, running to a downpipe at the side of the flight. Otherwise, you will end up with a saturated area in the flight where the rainwater falls off the edge of the plastic sheeting.

It is also worth installing guttering along the back of the shelter, with the water running into a soakaway or a rain-butt. Bolt the roof of the shed securely to the sides and then nail on the roofing felt. Two layers of a heavy duty mineralized brand are recommended. You can paint the upper surface white in order to reflect the heat of the sun. This will reduce the likelihood of the felt splitting, which would allow rainwater to penetrate to the roof.

You may want to fix plastic sheeting to the sides of the flight as well as to the roof. During the winter it can be particularly useful to cover in more of the flight, and you can make a number of secondary panels covered with plastic sheeting for this purpose. These should fit inside the existing wooden frames and be held in place by catches. They can then be removed or replaced according to the weather.

It is possible to improve the degree of insulation in the shelter by covering the inner surfaces of the framework with oil-tempered hardboard. Various materials, such as polystyrene or insulation quilting, can be placed in the space between the frame and the hardboard, although this is not really necessary as the air trapped in this gap will provide insulation.

The potential drawback of insulating the shelter is that you may be providing a hiding place for mice, so watch for any holes in the material. Although insulation is often only considered for the winter, it can also prove helpful in the summer months, as it will keep the interior temperature slightly lower than that outside.

It can be advantageous to have a power supply available. Heating, in the form of a tubular heater, can be supplied, provided that it is adequately screened with mesh so the birds cannot reach it. Cables must be protected in ducting, and any light will have to be screened with a wire mesh surround.

Since birds cannot recognize clear glass, you should cover the windows in the shelter with wire mesh. This will stop the birds from attempting to fly through what appears to be an opening and injuring themselves, perhaps fatally. As always, cover the cut strands of netting with battening. Take particular care in this instance not to break the glass when tapping the panel pins into the wooden surround.

The floor of the flight
The floor covering of the flight needs careful consideration. Here we examine the possible options.

Plant cover Unlike parrots, the majority of softbills will not damage growing vegetation. Plants will attract insects, which are vital for the successful rearing of chicks. Suitable plant cover in the aviary will also provide a good selection of nesting sites.

In the case of a small aviary, however, plants may not thrive, simply because of the soil conditions. Poor drainage can often be a problem, and waterlogged soil will cause plants to die back. A poorly designed planted flight can be difficult to keep clean with the result that birds are exposed to the risk of infection. Accumulated droppings and food particles rapidly turn mouldy, encouraging bacteria, which thrive in the damp conditions. If a severe outbreak of disease does occur, it is very difficult to clean the aviary thoroughly without digging out the top layer of soil.

It is possible, however, to devise a system which overcomes these problems, while retaining the advantages of the planted flight. In a big aviary, the plants can be set naturally into the ground, but in the smaller aviary it is better to grow plants in containers standing on paving stones.

Paving stones If you decide to use this system of cultivation, ensure that the floor of the flight is relatively flat. Remove the top 15cm (6in) of soil to form a base for a bed of mortar on which to lay the paving slabs. Check that the slabs ' are as level as possible, because any unevenness will be emphasized once the heavy pots are put in position.

Some of the plants often included in aviaries grow very rapidly and may almost take over the enclosure. Restricting their growth by planting them in pots and troughs saves a great deal of pruning. The amount of vegetation in the aviary will not be constant throughout the year, and it is useful to include a few annual plants. These too can be grown in pots or troughs.

The advantage of paving slabs is that droppings can be cleaned up easily. You can use a hose if you are careful, particularly if there is a slight incline for drainage purposes. You can make a drainage hole from a piece of narrow tubing set at ground level near the end of the flight.

During the breeding season, some birds may build their nests in an exposed part of the aviary. If this happens, cover part of the roof of the flight so that the nest does not become saturated with rainwater, which could result in the loss of a clutch of eggs. But remember that you will then have to water the plants, using a hose with caution.

Grass cover If your aviary is large enough, you may be able to keep a grass floor. It is better to use turves rather than seed since this way the grass will establish itself quite quickly. It is likely that you may have turves already available from when the aviary site was being cleared. Keep the turves well watered on a bed of soil, especially until they are established. One

Below: *Choose plants that will suit the size of the aviary flight. If they grow too vigorously, you may need to prune them. Here, conifers and clumps of bamboo provide useful nesting sites for breeding birds.*

reason for not using grass seed is that it may be dressed with toxic compounds which could harm birds eating it.

It is still a good idea to set some paving stones into the ground as these will permit you to enter on a regular basis without fear of damaging the grass. In most cases, even though you have plants in the aviary, you will still have to supply perches for the birds. Slabs can be stragetically placed under the main perches, where the bulk of the droppings will accumulate. This will make it easier to clean the aviary, since most of the droppings will be confined to specific parts.

Plants for the aviary
The choice of plants will be influenced to some extent by climatic factors. If you are in doubt about the suitability of a particular specimen, seek advice from a nursery. Some plants provide particularly good ground cover, often attracting a wealth of insects, which will be eaten by many softbills. Bushes tend to be more valuable as nesting sites. Climbers offer seclusion and may also be used for breeding purposes.

Ground cover Many annual plants can be grown in aviaries to provide ground cover. Among the most versatile are Nasturtiums (*Tropaeolum majus*). These do well

even in poor soil and, under these circumstances, tend to produce more flowers than leaves. There are various different types of nasturtiums, with the trailing varieties being especially useful in the aviary. They can be planted in any container and will grow rapidly, provided that the soil is not allowed to dry out. Nasturtiums will attract livefood to the aviary, particularly blackfly aphids which are eaten by many smaller softbills. Certain butterflies may also lay their eggs on nasturtium leaves, and the resulting caterpillars will be enjoyed by the birds.

Strawberries can now be raised from seed without difficulty, and the small alpine varieties are best for the aviary. The fruits will be eaten by many softbills, while others will be attracted to the various invertebrates among the leaves.

Some perennial plants can also be used to provide ground cover. These include various conifers, but check before you buy one of these plants, because some grow straight upwards and may rapidly become too large for the aviary. The dense, yet often rigid, structure of conifer bushes affords

Below: *The spacious flights of an extensive aviary housing a wide range of softbills. These are joined to a central birdroom with indoor flights for wintertime care.*

plenty of secluded nesting sites. These plants are evergreen and give good colour all year.

Shrubs

A number of fruiting shrubs are also frequently included in a planted aviary. Try to avoid any with sharp thorns, such as blackberries (although you can get a thornless variety of this plant). Elder (*Sambucus nigra*) grows freely, even in poor soil, and has attractive white flowers, followed in the autumn by edible berries. It is easy to establish and usually proves vigorous, but the main drawback of this plant is its rather unpleasant odour. Small elder bushes can often be found growing on waste sites, even in city centres, and they can be transplanted quite successfully.

One shrub which looks most attractive in the autumn is Pyracantha (*Pyracantha coccinea*). At this time it is covered in red berries, which members of the thrush family find particularly tasty. Like Elder, this plant can be trained quite easily, but its prominent sharp spines may be hazardous. Cotoneaster (*Cotoneaster* species) is probably a better option. It also has red berries, but lacks spines. One of the most popular climbers, often recommended for a planted aviary, is Russian Vine (*Polygonum baldschuanicum*). This is a dependable and profuse grower which, if left unchecked, can rapidly take over an aviary. Be sure to cut it back regularly. There is a danger that the weight of this climber may damage the aviary mesh, creating holes through which the birds may escape. Russian Vine produces creamy flowers in the summer before shedding its leaves during the autumn, at which stage the aviary mesh should be checked carefully for any holes.

Other climbing plants which produce attractive flowers are Honeysuckle (*Lonicera hensyii*), which has the added advantage of being an evergreen plant, and Clematis (*Clematis* species). There are many forms of the latter, but they may prove difficult to establish, preferring rather damp but sunny localities. It is therefore important to prevent the soil drying out, and covering the area close to the roots with a paving slab will help to trap moisture. The species known as *Clematis montana* is often recommended for aviaries. It flowers in early spring and requires little pruning.

Another early spring flowering shrub worth considering is Forsythia (*Forsythia intermedia*). This grows readily from cuttings. Vibernum (*Viburnum carlesi*) is also recommended, and produces its white circular clumps of flowers in the spring. It tends not to grow too large and the flowers will attract a wide range of insects.

Constraining factors

Local soil conditions will greatly affect your choice of plants unless you are growing them in tubs containing a suitable soil mix. Rhododendrons (*Rhododendron* species) are among the most spectacular of the flowering shrubs, but will not do well in soils containing lime. Choose one of the dwarf species for the aviary. In a large enclosure, these shrubs can look truly spectacular when in flower. Set rhododendrons in a peaty soil and keep this moist to help establish the plants.

Climatic factors will also have an effect on the choice of plants. In mild climates, you should be able to grow Passion Flowers (*Passiflora* species) outside throughout the year, but these plants are not hardy in temperate areas. If trained up a suitable small trellis, you may be able to bring the pot inside during the winter.

Flowering plants are especially valuable in aviaries housing nectivores. Fuchsias of various types will provide nectar for these birds and enable them to feed naturally; hummingbirds, for example, will hover in front of the flowers to feed.

The choice of plants is therefore very large. Even plants such as

runner beans can be of value in the aviary, as they will attract insects.

Planning the layout

Be sure to plan the layout carefully, so that you can derive maximum enjoyment from the natural appearance of the aviary. Put the climbers and taller plants around the back and sides of the aviary, leaving the central area relatively clear at the front, where you can use ground cover plants. Outside the aviary, you may want to screen the structure with fast-growing conifers such as Leyland Cypress (*Cupressocyparis leylandii*), or even clumps of Bamboo (*Sinarundinaria* species), both of which will give wind protection.

A pond

You may feel that you also want to incorporate a small pond so that the birds can bathe freely whenever they wish. Unfortunately, this is not generally recommended, because chicks, especially, may drown unless the water level is very low. However, very shallow water is a problem in hot weather, because the water will quickly evaporate and algal growth, stimulated by the sunshine, will contaminate the remaining water.

It will be difficult, if not impossible, to clean and empty the pond regularly without disturbing the birds. Therefore, unless you are able to supply a shallow

Above: *Although a small pond can be an attractive feature of a garden aviary, it may be difficult to keep clean. Take care to ensure that the aviary occupants, especially young chicks, cannot drown in the water.*

stream of clean running water, it is probably best not to attempt to provide a pond of any kind in the aviary. However, if you are keeping rails, you may want to sink a large plant-propagating tray into the floor, close to the door of the shelter. You can disguise the edges with suitable plants, and it will be easy to clean, simply by lifting it out and emptying it daily.

Birdrooms

Keeping softbills can prove an expensive hobby, particularly if you intend to overwinter the more delicate species in an outside aviary. A birdroom, which is simply an expansion of the basic shelter – although it may be constructed as a separate unit – will then become essential. This building will need to be well insulated. Keeping softbills in a warm, fairly humid environment where the air is stagnant will almost inevitably lead to cases of aspergillosis – a fungal disease which is virtually impossible to cure once established in the birds' airways (see also page 62).

An extractor fan is useful for improving the circulation of air, but be prepared for the initial cost of connecting an electrical supply to the aviary. The electrical cable may well have to be buried in a trench 45cm (18in) in depth, depending on local requirements. Clearly, the use of electricity out of doors can be very dangerous, so seek the advice of a qualified electrician before carrying out any work.

Heating

Today, there are many pieces of electrical equipment which can be of use to the softbill enthusiast. The most essential consideration will be a reliable and economic heater. Here we review some of the options available.

Tubular heaters, working on the convector principle, are probably the most widely used means of supplying heat in a birdroom. They are manufactured in various lengths and can be mounted either on the floor or, preferably, on a wall of the birdroom. The major advantage of these tubes is that they are effectively sealed units and, as a result, will not be affected by dust in the birdroom. Fan heaters, on the other hand, may actually stir up dust, because they provide such an efficient means of circulating air. Convector heaters tend to be less effective in this regard, with the air simply rising as it becomes warm. They can, however, be combined with a water tray in order to maintain the humidity level within the birdroom.

It is usual for the equipment to be connected to a thermostat. This will switch the heater on and off automatically, according to a predetermined temperature setting. In most cases, the thermostat should be set to turn on the heating if the temperature within the birdroom falls to 4.4°C (40°F), although a higher setting may be required for some species. If the structure is well insulated, heat loss from the building will be reduced and the heater will not come on so often.

It is best to choose a heater with a relatively high wattage. This is simply because in very bad weather a smaller model may be unable to cope. Although a higher wattage model will consume more power while it is actually producing heat, the thermostat will automatically switch it off once the predetermined temperature is reached. Therefore, it will not in fact be more costly to operate.

Conversely, during the summer months, particularly in warm climates, the birdroom may get too hot. It is possible to buy an extractor fan which operates with a thermostatic control, switching on automatically when temperatures rise above a certain level.

Paraffin (kerosene) heaters are not safe for use in a birdroom, and are in fact illegal in some parts of the world.

Perch heaters

Certain softbills are especially at risk from frostbite if they choose to roost in the flight where there is normally no heating. It is possible, however, to devise a system for warming the perches to protect the birds' toes from freezing conditions. Once set up, this is cheap to operate and a reliable way of ensuring that the birds do not succumb to the crippling after-effects of sub-zero temperatures.

The system is based on a method of warming pipes used by the chemical industry. The heating element is contained within a flexible tape and, under thermostatic control, produces a gentle warmth. The most durable heating tape has a plaited stainless steel exterior, which can be fixed to the perch using metal clips. The tape should be run along the undersurface of the perch, where it will keep the tips of the birds' toes warm. The rising heat will also warm the rest of the foot. A supply of about 15 watts per 30cm (1ft) is ideal, and there is no risk of the birds burning their feet since the heat is emitted evenly along the full length of the tape, eliminating the possibility of hot spots.

In order to avoid having to put in several lengths of tape, you may need to modify the arrangement of perches in the aviary. Ensure that one perch, under cover and running the full width of the flight, is positioned higher than the others. The birds will tend to roost here. Also, you can encourage birds to roost in the shelter at night by adjusting the inside perches so that they are even higher than those in the flight. It is also helpful, when you first place the birds in the aviary, to shut them in the shelter every night for several weeks. This should encourage them to continue to roost in there.

Lighting

During cold weather, the birds will convert more of the food they have eaten to energy in order to maintain their body temperature. In temperate areas, the coldest spells of weather tend to coincide with the shortest periods of day length. This means that the birds expend more energy on keeping warm but have a shorter feeding period. When provided with artificial light, however, they are able to continue eating for a longer time. This is clearly advantageous, especially for the smaller species, which are more vulnerable to hypothermia.

There are several ways of lighting a birdroom. You can use an ordinary tungsten light bulb and socket, although many aviculturists prefer strip lighting, particularly with a 'natural' fluorescent tube. This emits light of a 'balanced' spectrum close to that of sunlight, including some ultraviolet rays. The birds are then able to synthesize their own vitamin D , as happens in the wild. Since glass tends to filter out ultraviolet light, birds kept inside may be at risk from a deficiency of this vital vitamin, although it is usually also present in their food.

It is not necessary for you to switch the lights on and off in the birdroom, as this can be done automatically using dimming devices and time switches. Dimmers gradually reduce the light intensity over a period of a quarter of an hour or so. This ensures that the birds have time to find a perch

on which to roost, rather than being caught in another part of the aviary when the lights switch off suddenly. When purchasing a dimmer, check that it will also operate fluorescent tubes, since some models only operate with tungsten filament bulbs. Dimmers will also mimic dawn by increasing the light intensity in the morning.

The most sophisticated lighting controls actually respond to outside conditions, switching on the light if it becomes dark during a storm, for example. They work using a photo-electric cell fitted to a window.

Lighting in the birdroom can also be helpful to the aviculturist. Even on the shortest winter days, you will be able to check the birds carefully at any time, and you will be able to see to feed them. In any event, always try to avoid entering the aviary after dark. This may cause the birds to panic, and they may injure themselves as a result.

Ionizers

In the birdroom, during the winter months in particular, ventilation tends to be poor. Bacteria and other micro-organisms can then spread easily within the confined

Below: *To prevent birds fighting, several drinkers containing nectar are located around this aviary. A ball of nesting material is hanging from the roof at top right.*

air space. In order to overcome this problem, and to improve the environment within the birdroom generally, many softbill keepers now use an ionizer alongside existing heating and lighting facilities. Although most designs run on mains electricity, often fitting into a light socket, they are exceedingly cheap to operate. If necessary, some models can be run off a car battery.

The ionizer itself is in the form of a tube, at the end of which is a needle. Here, a perpetual stream of negative ions is produced, and these will precipitiate dirt and micro-organisms out of the atmosphere. The debris drops to the floor and can be easily wiped up with a damp mop or cloth.

The negative ions can also actually destroy harmful bacteria. Monitoring has shown that using an ionizer for one hour can reduce the atmospheric bacterial count by 90%. Although the introduction of ionizers to birdrooms is a relatively recent development, they have been used for many years with farm livestock. Their ease of installation, low operating cost and effectiveness make them well worth including as standard equipment in the birdroom.

Indoor planted aviaries

A tropical house, displaying a variety of softbills against a backdrop of exotic plants, is a popular feature at many zoos and bird gardens. Unfortunately, it is not possible to create a similar environment on a smaller scale so successfully at home. While a greenhouse or a conservatory attached to the house may appear to provide ideal conditions, this is rarely the case in practice.

As it is not possible to insulate a structure of this type, the large expanse of glass will cause the inside temperature to rise excessively in summer, while in winter heat will be lost very rapidly. In most cases, if the plants are to thrive, a temperature of about 15°C (59°F) is necessary. Humidity is important, but if ventilation is poor, moulds and fungi will spread rapidly, harming plants and birds.

You are more likely to succeed if you use a purpose-built aviary rather than if you adapt an existing glass structure. Block walls, with natural illumination provided by skylights and supplemented by artificial lighting as necessary, should help to control temperature excesses. The windows can be fitted with automatic opening and closing devices, such as are widely used in greenhouses. These will respond automatically to temperature changes within the structure. Painting exposed areas of glass with white paint will deflect the sun's rays during the summer, without seriously restricting light within the house.

You will need to screen exposed areas of glass to protect the birds. Bead curtains can be used to highlight the presence of a physical barrier if you do not want to cover the whole window with a netting frame. Certainly, windows should be adequately protected with mesh in order to exclude cats.

A different selection of plants can be included in a heated enclosure of this type, although the blooms of delicate flowering plants may be destroyed even by small birds such as honeycreepers. Again, devise a plan for the whole enclosure, using tall plants at the back and climbers to disguise any unsightly areas. Indoor aviaries rarely have grass, but you may want to consider synthetic turf, which can be used to cover a concrete floor, for example. This is available from many garden centres and, as it is washable, will not be difficult to keep clean.

Leave a clear area, free from plants, which is easily accessible for feeding. Put the food in several containers, because some birds become highly territorial, driving others away from the feeding site. Careful selection of your softbills should reduce the likelihood of such problems, but the birds' behaviour is likely to alter, especially once they are in breeding condition.

Feeding

These days, feeding softbills is relatively straightforward, and a wide range of diets is produced specifically for these birds. The situation has changed quite dramatically over the past few decades. Few softbill enthusiasts now prepare their own food mixtures as was once necessary before commercial diets become widely available. Several companies have invested heavily in research into the dietary requirements of these birds, to assist with the formulation of their brands of food. This has resulted in the production of several diets to suit the varying needs of different softbills. The better understanding of the feeding needs of softbills has, in turn, played an important part in the advancements made in the breeding of these birds.

Softbill diets

Softbill foods (sometimes called insectile or insectivorous foods) vary in content. Some have a higher level of oil than others, making them more suitable for the omnivorous and insectivorous species. This type of food does not suit frugivorous softbills which, in the wild, eat a diet with a low level of oil. Softbill mixtures are also graded, the coarser types being more suitable for larger birds.

Always read the feeding instructions on the packet. Loose softbill foods can be given sprinkled over fruit. You can also offer them in a separate food pot for birds such as tanagers, which will be able to eat the small pieces. The majority of brands can now be used straight from the packet, although some still need to be mixed with water. If so, add just enough to ensure that the food is crumbly, but not sloppy. Throw away any food left uneaten from the day before.

Pelleted softbill foods are a more recent innovation. These vary in size and are particularly valuable for softbills that cannot eat loose mixes because of their feeding habits. Typical examples are fruit pigeons and toucans, which will readily take to pelleted diets. Those brands which need to be soaked in water for 20 minutes or so prior to feeding tend to be the most palatable. Again, do not flood them: soak them in just enough cold water to cover them. You may find the pellets are sold as mynah food, but they will be quite acceptable to many other softbills.

Fruit

Feeding softbills is not entirely a matter of using prepared foods. You must offer fruit on a daily

Below: *A pair of Blue-naped Chlorophonias on their feeding dishes. Cleanliness is vital; wash all food containers every day.*

Above: *A varied diet plays an important part in the conditioning of softbills for breeding purposes. Prepare fresh food supplies daily.*

basis to most species. This even includes most of the insectivorous softbills, which eat fruit regularly. Feeding only commercial softbill food can cause problems, especially for frugivorous species, because it tends to be too rich and may cause liver disorders. If you are concerned about providing a suitable balance of fruit and commercial softbill food, observe the birds' feeding habits. They will almost certainly eat the fruit first, and if there is any left when you came to clean the food pot, you are feeding them too much. If no feeding guide is given with the food, start by offering roughly equal parts of fruit and softbill pellets mixed together.

Softbills will eat a wide range of fruits, and apple is often the most common kind provided. Use only dessert apples, because cooking apples tend to be too acid. Grapes are a particular favourite with many softbills. There is no need to remove the pips from the larger varieties, although you may need to cut them up. Small seedless grapes can be offered whole. Any pips that are swallowed will pass uneventfully through the birds' digestive tract, although in the case of some fruit-eating pigeons, the seeds will actually be digested in the gizzard.

You can maintain a constant supply of grapes throughout the

year by buying a large quantity when they are at their cheapest and deep freezing them. Check the grapes carefully, removing any with mould on their skins. Take them off their stalks and wash them thoroughly in a colander under running water. Leave the grapes to drain, then spread them on a clean tray and put them in the freezer. Once they are frozen, transfer the grapes to a clean plastic container. The advantage of first freezing the grapes on a tray is that they do not stick together, so you can remove small quantities at a time. If you have a number of softbills, it may be easier to weigh out batches of enough grapes to feed the birds for one day. Then freeze these portions in separate plastic bags. Stoned plums also freeze quite well, but apples become discoloured and their texture deteriorates.

The condition of the fruit used for feeding softbills is important. Bananas should be firm, but not under ripe, as this may cause digestive disturbances, especially in the more delicate species. For the same reason, oranges are not very popular with softbill keepers, although a small quantity will

41

Above: *A careful selection of plants can provide your aviary birds with fruits in season. Here, a Grey-headed Parrotbill feeds on berries, which are very popular with many softbills. Some of the domesticated varieties of fruiting plants, such as thornless blackberries, are suitable for inclusion in flights. You can deep freeze berries and other fruits.*

provide valuable Vitamin C. It is interesting that, unlike other birds, some frugivorous species, such as the Red-vented Bulbul, are unable to manufacture Vitamin C in their bodies. This inability has probably developed because in the wild their diet would include adequate quantities of this vitamin.

Softbills enjoy a variety of fruits, but these need not always be fresh. Canned fruit (in natural juice rather than syrup) can be added to the food mixture. You can also use dried fruits, but soak them overnight in a bowl of water then rinse them before feeding them to the birds. Larger fruits, such as dried figs or apricots, should be cut into smaller pieces for most species. The inclusion of dried fruits in the diet is especially valuable during the winter, since

Food suitable for softbills

You will need to provide a mixture of foods to keep your softbills in good health. A basic diet usually consists of fruit and softbill food, supplemented with livefood. Take care to ensure that all livefoods, such as maggots, are free from potential diseases, such as botulism. Nectar plays an important part in the diet of so-called nectivorous softbills, notably hummingbirds and sunbirds. As with the other foods, provide a fresh supply each day and wash all feeding containers thoroughly.

Fruits for softbills. From top left: Orange, apple, raisins and grapes.

they have a higher calorific value than fresh fruit. In fact, fruit tends to be a poor source of nutrients, consisting largely of water.

The preparation of the food depends upon the species you are keeping. Generally, having washed the fruit, it is best to chop it into small chunks. Some birds, such as toucans, tend to consume their food whole, although they may tear large items to pieces, holding them against the perch. Fruit for sunbirds should be finely diced, because they are not able to use their beaks to bite off chunks. In the wild, they would normally live on small berries that can be swallowed whole.

Livefood

While commercial softbill foods help to provide a balanced diet,

the birds will prefer insects, which they will eat instinctively. Unfortunately, one of the major problems in breeding softbills is not persuading the birds to lay and hatch their chicks but, rather how to provide adequate livefood to ensure that the young are reared successfully.

Although prepared softbill food is more nutritious, it will not supplant the parent birds' natural instinct to feed their chicks on insects. This reflects the need for a high protein level in the diet of the young softbill in order to support its growth. Vitamins, such as D_3, are also necessary. This particular vitamin facilitates the absorption of calcium and helps to regulate the calcium/phosphorus ratio. A deficiency will result in skeletal deformities in the young birds.

Sunbird   Toucan

Above: *The shape of its beak can be a clue to a bird's feeding habits. The relatively long, thin bill characteristic of both sunbirds and hummingbirds is ideal for probing within flowers for pollen grains and nectar. It also enables the birds to catch small insects which are attracted to flowering plants.*

Above: *In* Ramphastos *toucans, the bill is elongated, broad and brightly coloured. Its lightness and strength enable the bird to reach and pluck ripening fruits from branches, and grab small mammals and similar creatures that it may encounter. Toucans have narrow, fringed tongues.*

From top left: Nectar paste, powder, universal food, and mynah pellets.

These are mealworms, as received from specialist livefood suppliers.

Unfortunately, livefood tends to be unbalanced in nutritional terms, and may need to be supplemented. Several kinds of livefoods are bred in large numbers at special farms. Indeed, because of the time involved in catching or cultivating your own, you may prefer to opt for commercially produced supplies. But again, variety is important.

Collecting livefood Some birdkeepers like to catch their own livefood. Trawling the grass with a muslin bag will catch some invertebrates that can then be tipped into the aviary. For a more sophisticated approach, you can invest in one of the insect traps favoured by entomologists. These operate at night, and the trapped insects can then be offered to the birds the following day. However, if you have any cause to suspect that insecticides have been used in the area, it is probably best not to use a trap, for fear of poisoning your birds.

You may be able to find spiders in your garden. These are popular with many softbills, especially the smaller birds. Since they have no hard outer covering in most cases, spiders are useful for feeding to young softbills. Aphids are also highly valued for this purpose. You can often collect a quantity by firmly tapping a leaf into a clean plastic tub. Plants in the aviary will attract aphids and other invertebrates, and during the summer months there should be a ready supply.

Woodlice can be a useful source of livefood, especially for the more omnivorous softbills. They can be found quite easily under stones and rotting wood. However, as with many other livefoods, woodlice will rapidly escape in the aviary unless they are adequately contained. A smooth-sided vessel is ideal for this purpose. Make sure that while the sides of the container delay the escape of the woodlice, they do not prevent the softbills from reaching them easily. The birds will soon come to

recognize this container and will rush to feed from it. Many softbills become very tame when offered livefood on a regular basis. Shamas, for example, will often start feeding from the container before you have placed it on the floor of the aviary.

Supplies of wild livefood tend to be rather seasonal. Snails abound during the spring and summer, but become scarce later in the year, especially after a period of hot, dry weather. Their size renders them unsuitable for many species of softbills, but they are especially popular with thrushes, which will break the shell on the floor of the aviary.

In the later part of the summer, ants' nests often contain whitish 'eggs', which are in fact pupae containing immature ants. These are another valuable food for chicks. One simple means of harvesting the eggs is to lay a cloth on the ground with its edges folded inwards, and then tip the nest into the centre of the cloth. The adult ants will start to move the cocoons to the shade provided by the folds, where they can be easily collected. If possible, harvest the cocoons from several nests so that you do not harm the colony. In some areas, such as parts of Australia, it may be best not to use ants 'eggs' as you may inadvertently introduce certain termites that will attack the woodwork of the aviary.

Caterpillars can often be collected during the summer months, but avoid any with hairy skins. The birds will not eat this kind, because the hairs are likely to cause irritation. Make sure that you only take common species, since many butterflies are becoming quite scarce.

Earthworms These are a particularly valuable source of protein, but keep them on a bed of damp grass for several days before offering them to the birds. This will ensure that the contents of the earthworms' guts are voided, thus reducing the risk of the bird being harmed by the decaying vegetation on which the earthworm feeds. If you are collecting earthworms from the garden, avoid digging near manure heaps because of the heavy organic contamination.

During the summer, earthworms may appear to be less numerous, but you should still be able to obtain a regular supply. Put some vegetable matter, such as potato peelings, in a shaded part of the garden, covered with hessian sacking, and keep this well watered. This attracts earthworms to the surface, even when the surrounding soil is very dry.

Unfortunately, you cannot guarantee the size of the earthworms you dig up. This is not a problem for many species, but with smaller softbills, you may have to cut the worms up, which is an unpleasant task. It may be better therefore to obtain a supply from a breeder offering worms graded in size. Apart from earthworms, you can also use redworms which are bred for angling enthusiasts.

Maggots Maggots are another fishing bait acceptable as livefood for softbills, but do not buy the ones which have been dyed. Maggots are the larval form of flies, with the name 'gentles' being given to the blowfly maggots. You can breed maggots very easily, especially during the warmer months of the year, simply by leaving meat outside, in a covered bowl. Flies will be attracted and will lay eggs, which will hatch very rapidly into maggots. These feed on the putrid meat and pupate within a few days, depending on the environmental temperature. Harvest the maggots quickly, therefore,lifting them out of the meat with tweezers.

In view of their unsavoury feeding habits, it is vital to clean maggots before giving them to softbills. If this is not carried out properly, the birds are liable to succumb to diseases, notably botulism. Transfer the maggots to a tub containing bran, and leave them there for at least three days. They will then ingest the bran, which is harmless, and pass the putrid meat out of their system.

Below: *An American Robin feeding on an earthworm. Livefood forms a vital part of the softbill diet; provide insects and invertebrates when there are chicks in the nest.*

Sawdust is sometimes recommended in place of bran, but may itself prove toxic to the birds when they eat the maggots.

It is important to keep the immature flies cool once they have pupated, otherwise they will rapidly emerge as adults from their cocoons. However, adult flies are also a valuable source of food for insectivorous species such as flycatchers. In order to give the birds maximum opportunity to catch them, offer the flies in the following way. Tip the pupae into a jar, place a muslin cover over the top and hold this in position with a rubber band. Cut two or three small holes in the muslin, just large enough to let the flies squeeze through once they have hatched and their wings are dry. The birds will then be able to swoop on the insects as they leave the jar through the small holes. This ensures that only a few can escape from the jar at one time, increasing the likelihood that they will be eaten by the birds.

Fruit flies A similar technique can be used for fruit flies (*Drosophila*). These are especially valuable for smaller nectivores, such as hummingbirds, and should be offered on a regular basis. You can buy a starter culture and breed the flies easily, provided that they are kept at about 23°C (73°F). Although traditionally offered banana skins, which sustain the flies and provide a breeding ground, you may prefer to use a culture medium. This usually comes as a powder, which you simply mix with water, and which sustains the flies without giving off any odour.

Special feeders are also available, which double as breeding enclosures for the fruit flies. Place their food at the bottom of the container and restrain the flies by turning the lid to block off the small exit hole at the top. Then transfer the container to the aviary and open the exit hole. The flies will escape, a few at a time, and will be eaten by the birds as they emerge from the hole.

In a warm birdroom, fruit flies will almost certainly establish themselves as a free-flying population, especially if you leave a bucket of banana skins for them. Fruit flies adapt to any fruit, but banana is best because it does not quickly become mouldy like other fruits, but simply turns black and shrivels up. However, in some areas of the world, fruit flies are outlawed because of the damage they could cause the fruit industry.

Fruit flies have become a popular subject for research study because of their genetic adaptability. One effect of this is the development of a wingless strain, with tiny vestigial wings. This variety is especially useful for birds that catch small insects found on the ground, rather than in the air. Small tanagers, for example, will greedily consume these fruit flies. Being unable to fly, there is also less chance of the flies escaping. Ask your local dealer about these fruit fly strains.

Crickets and locusts The size of the livefood will affect its usefulness, but this problem can be overcome to some extent, in the case of crickets. These are now quite widely available and, like other commercially developed livefoods, can be acquired by mail order. Crickets are normally sold on the basis of their size, and tiny hatchlings can be given even to the smallest nectivores.

You can of course rear crickets, either to feed to larger softbills or in order to establish your own breeding culture. Although this is not particularly expensive, it will be time consuming. An acrylic fish tank equipped with the type of lid sold for housing reptiles can accommodate crickets. The lid has a hole for an electric light bulb fitting plus a ventilation panel. Line the bottom of the tank with newspaper, fill some clean margarine tubs with damp sand and place them on top of the newspaper. These will act as receptacles for the eggs, and should therefore be at least 7.5cm (3in) in depth. You will be able to recognize female crickets quite easily, because their abdomens are relatively pointed in comparison with the males'.

Feeding crickets is quite straightforward. They simply need a dish of flour and a supply of fresh grass. You may prefer to plant small trays with budgerigar seed. This germinates quite quickly and you can then put a tray in the tank with the crickets. If you keep the tray watered, the crickets will have a constant supply of greenfood. A moist piece of sponge will act as a water reservoir. Alternatively, you can provide a shallow dish of water, but only for adult crickets as hatchlings are likely to drown.

A high level of humidity is especially important once the eggs have been laid, and the surface of the sand must be kept moist. If the eggs are kept at about 27°C (81°F), the hatchlings will start to emerge through the sand within a fornight or so. They mature quite rapidly, with the entire life cycle taking about six weeks. Before offering the crickets to the softbills, it is a good idea to put them in a plastic

Below: *This automatic feeder for mynah pellets is useful in an aviary. Make sure it has a wide base so that the flow of pellets does not become jammed. Clean separate components every day.*

container and leave them in the refrigerator for a short time. This lowers their level of activity and the birds can catch them more easily.

Locusts are also eaten by some softbills although, generally, they are less widely used than crickets. Adult locusts are significantly larger than crickets and their life cycle is also longer, making them more expensive to buy. They can be looked after and bred in a similar way to crickets, with the young hoppers starting to breed at about eight weeks, having undergone a series of moults beforehand. Humidity is important at this stage, to ensure that the old skin is shed easily.

Mealworms The hard outer casing of the mealworm gives this larva of the meal beetle (*Tenebrio molitor*) its distinctive banded appearance. Mealworms are readily eaten by most softbills but, because of this covering, some species, and especially young chicks, may have difficulty digesting them. In nutritional terms, they tend to be low in calcium and this deficiency is likely to be exacerbated if they are kept in bran. This is because the phytic acid in bran handicaps the absorption of calcium. The food value of mealworms can in fact vary quite widely, depending upon the culture in which they are kept. The best results are likely to be achieved if they are fed on chicken meal, which is itself a balanced diet.

As mealworms can escape quite easily from an open container, they are best kept in a clean margarine or ice-cream tub with a lid. Punch ventilation holes through the top but make sure these are not large enough to permit the mealworms to escape. Put a generous layer of chicken meal in the container (say, at least 10cm/4in) and then tip in the mealworms. Put in some slices of apple to provide moisture without causing moulds to develop. You will need to replace the apple when it dries up.

It is important when you buy mealworms by post not to leave

them in their shipping container for any length of time, even if they have been fed. Closely confined, the mealworms will generate considerable heat and will 'sweat', leading to high losses.

Once you have transferred them to their permanent container, move the mealworms to a cool spot in order to slow down their development. Ultimately, however, some of the larvae will pupate, becoming inert and wrapped in whitish, comma-shaped cocoons. These will hatch into adult meal beetles, which are dark and unmistakable in appearance. The adult beetles will, in turn, lay eggs in the substrate. They hatch after about six weeks, and the tiny larvae grow through a series of successive moults. The hard casing of the mealworm is replaced during the moulting period, and the mealworm becomes temporarily whitish in appearance. At this stage you can safely feed them to all softbills, since they are soft-bodied.

Generally, mealworms start to pupate when they reach a length of about 3cm (1.2in). Recently, suppliers have started to grade them on the basis of their size. The smaller mealworms, often described as 'mini', are younger and tend to be more expensive. These are good for feeding to smaller softbills.

Above: *An Indian Blue-throated Flycatcher enjoying a mealworm. These invertebrates are available from specialist suppliers, but may be too large for smaller softbills.*

Whiteworms Another livefood of considerable value for the smaller softbill is the whiteworm (*Enchytraeus*). Again, whiteworms can be obtained in the form of a starter pack, with the worms being split into groups that will ultimately develop into colonies. Even when fully grown, whiteworms are tiny, being little more than 1cm (0.4in) long.

You can keep whiteworms in a variety of containers, but a clean margarine tub with holes in the lid for ventilation is best. Fill the tub with damp sterile peat. Wholemeal bread, moistened with a little milk, will provide adequate sustenance for the whiteworms. Use a pencil to make several holes in the peat, and put a little bread in each one. Then divide the whiteworms into the same number of clumps as there are holes, put them on the bread and cover them over with peat. It is best to arrange the holes in a set pattern so that you know where they are. You can then remove any leftover bread from each 'colony' before it turns sour and replace it with a fresh batch.

The temperature for culturing whiteworms is important. About

20°C (68°F) seems ideal. You may need to spray the surface of the peat very carefully in order to prevent it from drying out. After about a month, the colonies should be thriving sufficiently to enable you to harvest some of the whiteworms.

The simplest method of separating them from the food and peat is to use a bowl of water. With forceps, tease out a clump of whiteworms and drop them into the water. The worms will float, while the debris will sink to the bottom. You should then be able to scoop them out quite easily with a strainer.

It is advisable to set up a number of cultures before the start of the breeding season, so that by the time the chicks hatch you have sufficient whiteworms to meet their parents' demands. Unlike mealworms, it is not possible to purchase whiteworms in sufficient quantity for direct feeding to the birds, so culturing is essential.

Foods of animal origin Various other foods of animal origin can be useful for feeding to softbills. Many of the larger softbills appreciate raw mince, and freezer packs are available from supermarkets. Choose one of the free-flow brands if possible so that you can take out the amount of mince you need without having to thaw out a solid chunk of meat or hack pieces from a frozen block. Low-fat brands are preferable, especially for birds such as toucans, which may be adversely affected by high levels of dietary fat. The build-up of fatty deposits on the walls of their arteries, giving rise to atherosclerosis, may be directly linked to excessively high levels of fat in their diet.

Mince and other meats are deficient in various respects, notably in Vitamin A and calcium. Therefore, some softbill keepers prefer to offer dead day-old chicks. These are available from hatcheries, being surplus to requirements. Chicks are usually only fed to the larger, more carnivorous softbills, such as hornbills. Offer them whole and only give a few at a time. If frozen, allow them to thaw out thoroughly before feeding them to the birds, and never re-freeze any packs which have warmed up.

Laboratory rodents are also sometimes used as softbill food. The most common are newborn mice, known as 'pinkies'. These can be obtained frozen from specialist livefood suppliers and are particularly valuable when the softbills have chicks in the nest. Adult mice are really only suitable for the largest species, although even toucans will consume them on occasion.

Nectar foods

Several balanced nectar diets are now available to cater for the needs of hummingbirds, sunbirds and other nectivores. Indeed, preparing their food is very straightforward, especially in the case of powdered nectar mixes. Using the measuring spoon that is usually provided, mix a set number of spoonsful with water and stir until the powder has completely dissolved. In most cases, this will be sufficient for a pair of birds without being wasteful. It is not easy to prepare your own mixture for just a few nectivores, since measuring the ingredients accurately can be difficult and time consuming. Proprietary nectar foods are not especially cheap. However, dietary imbalances, leading to the condition of gout for example, are rarely encountered in birds fed with commercially prepared diets, and breeding results tend to be superior to those of nectivores fed on home-made nectar foods.

Avoid sudden changes in the diet of nectivores. This can lead to bacterial changes in the gut, giving rise to the condition known as enterotoxaemia. When you are buying a bird, therefore, always ask for details of its diet, and follow these instructions carefully during the early stages. You can then gradually introduce a new nectar mixture, offering it alongside the usual solution. In this way, the bird can adapt gradually to a new diet without fear of intestinal disturbances.

You will need to use nectar feeders for the birds. These vary in design, but all have a spout through which the birds obtain the nectar. Tinted glass bottles are widely used. They are filled from the top, and work using a rubber bung and suction pressure to prevent the nectar flowing out of the spout. The angle of the spout is not especially important, but most are horizontal. The area around the opening is invariably red, since this colour is known to attract nectivores, which in the wild show a distinct preference for red flowers.

The major drawback of a glass container is that it will break easily if dropped, and may crack in hot water. You may therefore prefer to use plastic drinkers, but take care when cleaning these that the interior does not become badly scratched. If this happens, bacteria and fungi can become established in the pitted surface, proving harmful to the birds.

Cleanliness is vital when dealing with nectivores. Be sure to clean the drinkers properly every day. You may be able to buy a special cleaning brush with the drinkers, but if not, use a bottle brush to clean the spout and interior.

Colour food
Certain softbills, notably those with any red plumage, may lose colour over successive moults and become rather pale. The rare Scarlet Cock of the Rock (*Rupicola peruviana*) is one example, while another species more likely to be encountered by the average softbill keeper is the Scarlet-chested Sunbird.

Early attempts to restore the natural coloration of these birds relied heavily on carrot juice and powdered red pepper, both of which contain natural colouring agents and can affect the depth of coloration of the birds' plumage.

Above: *A female Blue-chinned Sapphire Hummingbird sipping nectar from a specially designed feeding bottle. Hummingbirds invariably feed on the wing, hovering in front of the feeding vessel. However, it is better to locate containers for other softbills close to perches so that the birds do not scatter food on the floor.*

Left: *Nectar is the main item in the diet of sunbirds, as well as hummingbirds. Here, a cock Mariqua Sunbird feeds on an erica flower. Caring for these birds in captivity is quite straightforward, using specially formulated artificial nectar preparations. They also need a steady supply of livefood.*

Today, however, synthetic derivatives with greater potency are available in various forms. A soft food containing the colouring agent is suitable for some species. This can be used as a softbill diet and sprinkled over fruit. Alternatively, you can buy soluble preparations which are added to the drinking water.

Colour food in either form is normally not given until just before the bird starts to moult. At this time the new plumage receives a blood supply, which provides the means of transporting the colouring agent to the point of growth. Here it will be incorporated into the developing feathers, thus restoring brightness and depth of colour to the plumage. Colour food is offered right through the moulting phase and for a short time afterwards, so that any feathers which are late in developing will not emerge significantly paler than the others.

Make sure you read the instructions on the packet carefully. Overdosing is clearly not recommended, as this can tarnish the appearance of the plumage until the next moult. One of the earliest signs of overdosing is a change in the colour of the droppings, which usually take on a reddish hue. Feeding certain fruits may have a similar effect, so bear this in mind if you offer cherries or black grapes, for example.

Unless you wish to exhibit your softbills (see pages 64-65), it is not essential to use a colour food. However, some breeders believe that birds that are paler than normal through a lack of colour feeding may be less keen to reproduce, but so far this has not been proved conclusively.

Breeding

More softbills are being bred now than at any time in the past. The results in some instances are quite phenomenal: for example, a German aviculturist's collection of hummingbirds successfully produced more than 40 chicks in one breeding season. A better understanding of nutritional requirements has certainly played an important part in these successes, but other factors are also involved and these are dealt with in this section.

Sexing softbills

Many softbills cannot be paired up with certainty on the basis of differences in appearance between the sexes. This was a major handicap in the past, but now, even with species as small as barbets, it is possible to sex the birds reliably. The most commonly used method is known as 'surgical sexing'. This technique, as its name suggests, is invasive, and must be carried out by a veterinarian. It involves passing a laparoscope through a tiny incision in the abdominal wall in order to inspect the gonads. The bird is usually given a general anaesthetic, preferably gas, because this makes recovery much quicker.

In skilled hands, surgical sexing presents little danger to a healthy bird. The veterinarian may occasionally use a local anaesthetic if there is concern about the bird's general state of health. Indeed, laparoscopy sexing can also be useful for diagnostic purposes. Infection of the air-sacs with the fungus disease aspergillosis can be recognized by this means, even though the condition is normally difficult to confirm in a live bird. If you suspect that your softbill is ill in any way, mention this to the veterinarian right at the start, before any anaesthetic is administered.

There are other methods of sexing softbills, but these tend not to be as reliable, nor so freely available. They can be useful though, in the case of very small birds. Faecal steroid analysis involves testing the bird's droppings for the relative levels of sex hormones. It operates on a ratio basis, which tends to reduce its accuracy at present.

The most worthwhile of these laboratory methods is undoubtedly chromosomal karyotyping, which is based on study of the chromosomes present in the cell nuclei. One pair of chromosomes, known as the 'sex chromosomes', is distinctive. In the female, this pair, known as ZY, has one chromosome considerably shorter than the other. There is no such difference in the cock bird's chromosomes, which are known as ZZ. This means of sexing, although costly, is accurate right from the hatching stage. It is, however, technically demanding, especially since birds' chromosomes tend to be more fragile than those of mammals.

Sexing services are often advertised in avicultural magazines. In the case of surgical sexing, your veterinarian will know who carries out this procedure in your area. Far more veterinarians are now equipped for this task. Make the necessary appointment and ask if there are any particular instructions. You may, for example, have to withhold food from the bird overnight. Post-operative care tends to be relatively minimal, and the plumage around the incision soon regrows.

Breeding guidelines

The breeding habits of softbills are surprisingly diverse, but in order to breed any of these birds successfully you need to follow a few basic guidelines. On the whole, most species will be reluctant to nest if their surroundings are unsatisfactory. It is certainly no coincidence that the best breeding results are usually obtained from softbills housed in relatively large planted aviaries. In this semi-natural environment, insect life flourishes and the birds can select their own nesting sites.

Breeding softbills requires a degree of constraint on the part of the owner. Although the aviary may look more attractive with several birds in it, breeding tends to be less effective in a communal aviary. The best results generally occur when pairs are housed on their own. A few species, such as Zosterops, do better if kept in small groups, but they are the exception. Furthermore, once the chicks hatch, there is less competition for livefood if the breeding pair is housed on its own.

Nevertheless, you should buy at least four birds of any species, because when they have been sexed you may find that you have only one hen and three cocks. At least with four birds there is a greater chance of having a pair. Compatibility is an important factor, and with four birds you will be able to change around potential partners if necessary.

You may have to do this with *Ducula* fruit pigeons, for example. Cock birds can sometimes be very aggressive towards certain hens, but by moving partners around, you should find a compatible pair. The ideal solution is to introduce all four birds into the aviary simultaneously, wait until two birds pair up and then move them to separate accommodation.

If possible, introduce the birds to each other before the breeding period begins. It is quite usual for softbills to become more aggressive when they are in breeding condition, and they also tend to become increasingly territorial at this time. For this reason, you may have to remove some birds from a mixed collection if they are being persecuted.

If you do have the misfortune to lose one member of a breeding pair, having other birds of the

Below: *Many softbills will build their own nests in a well-planted aviary. This female Bay-headed Tanager has built a nest in a climbing convolvulus plant. Try not to disturb breeding birds.*

same species means you may have a ready replacement available. This will save time and trouble, since a newly imported bird cannot be expected to settle immediately and start breeding in unfamiliar surroundings. In fact, a newcomer would almost certainly have to be kept apart from its intended companion, which might otherwise, in its ardour, severely harass it at this time of year. This is especially likely when introducing a hen to a cock bird already in top breeding condition.

Breeding behaviour
The signs of breeding condition do vary somewhat, depending on the species. Cock shamas, for example, tend to sing more readily and usually become more active. Certain species have an obvious courtship display. The *Ducula* fruit pigeons bow and jump up and down on the perch, uttering a deep throaty call. Hens typically become more inquisitive; hummingbirds will often attempt to pluck hairs from your head for nest building.

Providing nesting facilities
It is well worth providing a number of artificial nesting sites. Pigeons, for example, will need a tray-like nesting area; mynahs use tree hollows or nestboxes. For touracos and other platform nesters, you can construct a plywood tray with 7.5cm (3in) edges. Fix this securely to one of the aviary uprights, preferably under cover in the flight, although some birds may prefer to nest in the shelter.

It is a good idea to offer a choice of nesting sites, particularly if the birds have not bred before in your care. Other nesting sites can be made from a plastic garden sieve, tied firmly in place with a loop of wire, or even a hanging basket. However, a basket must be suspended quite rigidly, so that it does not tip when a bird lands.

If the basket hangs by chains, it is a good idea to cover these with lengths of hosepipe so that the birds do not get caught up in the links. It is possible to construct a

wire basket using aviary netting, but there is a danger that any sharp ends of mesh might break the eggs.

Nesting boxes are useful for breeding those softbills that normally nest in tree holes. Mynahs will often adopt a standard parakeet nestbox, but check that the entry hole is wide enough to admit them easily. This applies especially to the larger species, such as hill mynahs. You may need access to the nestbox at some stage while the birds are breeding. It is best if the box has a removable lid and, if possible, a side inspection hatch. If there is no side hatch, do not position the nestbox too high in the flight or you will not be able to lift the lid.

Some tanagers may prefer a slightly different type of nestbox with a semi-open front. These birds also build their nests in an open wicker basket, although sometimes they simply prefer to weave a nest in the aviary vegetation. The dense foliage of Box (*Buxus sempervirens*) is ideal for this purpose.

Nest building
The extent of nest building again depends on the species. Some softbills will weave ornate nests in the aviary vegetation, whereas others will be satisfied with an untidy tangle of twigs laid on a ready made nesting platform. Hornbills tend to have the most specialized requirements, with the females of most species being sealed in behind a wall of mud until the chicks have hatched.

A number of softbills, ranging from barbets to tits, will actually use nestboxes and baskets for roosting in at night. You cannot, therefore, assume that reproductive activity is imminent, simply because the birds are occupying the nesting sites. However, once they start looking for nesting material, the chances of breeding are increased.

Not all softbills will take the nesting material you provide. Toucans and barbets, for example,

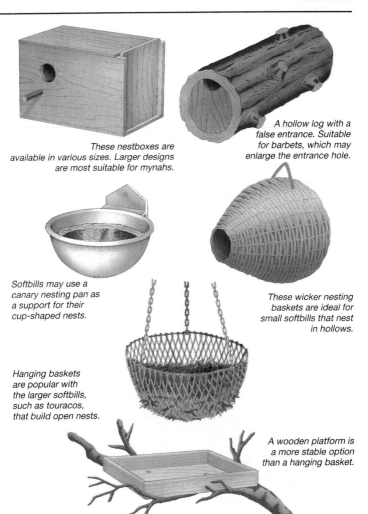

These nestboxes are available in various sizes. Larger designs are most suitable for mynahs.

A hollow log with a false entrance. Suitable for barbets, which may enlarge the entrance hole.

Softbills may use a canary nesting pan as a support for their cup-shaped nests.

These wicker nesting baskets are ideal for small softbills that nest in hollows.

Hanging baskets are popular with the larger softbills, such as touracos, that build open nests.

A wooden platform is a more stable option than a hanging basket.

Below: *A wire mesh support for the nests of larger birds, such as touracos. Position these platforms in a secluded part of the aviary.*

Above: *Suitable nesting receptacles for softbills. Even if you provide a choice of artificial sites, many birds prefer to construct their own nests in a well-planted aviary. Offering a choice of nesting containers and giving the birds a sense of security are vital to enhance the likelihood of breeding success. Avoid placing the nesting containers in an exposed position, since the birds will simply ignore them. Check also that boxes and baskets are held firmly in position, so that there is no risk of them collapsing, which may cause loss of eggs or chicks.*

55

generally prefer to make their own wood chips, using their beaks. Fruit pigeons, being typical of their family, will construct a loose nest with a few twigs, while mynahs and other starlings will collect almost anything to build a fairly bulky and untidy nest in their chosen box.

Most species require a wide variety of nesting material. Strands of horse hair, dry moss and even teased out hamster bedding will all be used by smaller birds. Hay may seem an obvious choice, but this can turn mouldy quite easily and, particularly within the confines of a nestbox, could prove harmful to the birds.

Those species that build cup shaped nests often appreciate a supply of moulted feathers, which they use to make a soft lining in the centre of the nest. Try to provide dry twigs for platform nest builders because fresh cut wood may turn mouldy, especially once it has been soiled by the chicks' droppings. Give toucans and barbets short lengths of softwood battening, which they will break into pieces with their beaks. Some owners put peat in the bottom of nestboxes, but this invariably turns rather dry and dusty and tends to be scratched out by the birds.

Incubation and rearing
Once you see that a pair of softbills have started nesting activities, leave them alone as much as possible. Disturbances may cause the birds to leave the nest and, although they may not

Below: *An African White-eye, or Zosterops, feeding her chicks. The first few days after hatching, and the fledging period, are the most crucial periods in the life of a young softbill. An inadequate diet, notably a shortage of suitable livefood, is the most common cause of early losses of chicks.*

actually desert it, the eggs will rapidly chill and may fail to hatch.

The vast majority of softbills become highly insectivorous during the rearing period, and it is important to make provision for this well in advance to cater for the needs of the chicks. Set up suitable cultures in the spring, before the breeding period commences (see pages 44-48). If possible, try to offer other foods apart from mealworms, especially in the early stages when the chicks have just hatched. This is because the young birds will have difficulty coping with the relatively indigestible body covering of these larvae.

Without livefood, it is most unlikely that the chicks will be reared successfully, although fruit pigeons and doves are an exception to this rule. Instead of relying on insects as a source of protein, these birds produce a protein-rich secretion known as crop milk, which nourishes the chicks through the early stages. This evolutionary development is perhaps the main reason why the pigeon family is so successful, managing to breed even in the centre of cities where it would be difficult to obtain sufficient insects.

Eggshells on the floor of the aviary may be one of the first signs of successful hatching. Often, the incubation period does not begin until the second or third egg has been laid, so that all the chicks tend to hatch at more or less the same time. At this stage keep any disturbance to an absolute minimum, but provide livefood several times a day to ensure that the adult birds have a constant supply. Assuming all goes well, the young softbills will develop quite quickly. Once they leave the nest, the parents continue to feed them until they are fully independent. At this point, you can remove them to separate quarters.

Banding
Some owners like to band their birds for identification purposes. There are two types of bands:

open and closed. A closed band must be fixed on the leg while the bird's toes are small enough to fit through it. However, it is not worth the risk of disturbing the parent birds to fit a band of this type on the chicks. An open band is a better choice, as this can be put on the leg at any stage. Plastic open bands can be used to identify individual adult birds as well as recently fledged chicks. Fit the band immediately above the foot, making sure that it can move freely up and down. Close it carefully so that there is no danger of the bird getting caught up in the aviary netting. These bands are produced in various sizes, so check that you have the correct size for the species concerned.

Breeding problems
The greatest risk during the laying period is that the hen may become egg bound, but this is a rare occurrence with softbills. An affected hen will suddenly appear ill and will soon be unable to perch. On close examination, you may be able to feel the egg which is causing the obstruction, and see the contractions in the vent. Move the hen without delay to a warm environment with a temperature of around 32°C (90°F). If there is no improvement within a couple of hours, seek veterinary advice as this condition may rapidly prove fatal. Your veterinarian has a choice of several treatments, ranging from an injection to surgery, and these are usually successful, provided that you seek help quickly.

The rearing phase is the most crucial period, especially the first few days after hatching. Many failures can be attributed to an inadequate or unsuitable supply of livefood. This may also be a contributory factor if adult birds consume their own chicks – such is their instinct to obtain livefood at this time.

Once you suspect the chicks have hatched, watch the area around the nest closely, because occasionally you will find a chick

Above: *An artificial nesting site for softbills that prefer to nest on the ground. The entrance to this hollow log has been partially filled with cement so that the interior is more secluded. Site such boxes in a sheltered area for best results.*

Below: *In the wild, ground nesting softbills, such as pittas, are clearly vulnerable to predators. In an aviary, they often go to great lengths to conceal their nests, as shown here. Avoid disturbing the nests of these nervous birds.*

on the floor of the aviary. If it has fallen out by accident (by getting caught up on the adult's foot as it leaves the nest, for example), you may be able to replace it successfully. Even if the chick appears inert and lifeless, hold it in your hand for a few moments. Young birds can be surprisingly robust and may start showing signs of life even when they appear dead. If the chick revives, quietly approach the nest and, hopefully, the sitting parent will leave as you draw near. Replace the chick with minimum disturbance and offer the parent birds some livefood to distract their attention. They should return to the nest soon afterwards.

Nests containing chicks may be deserted by their parents for a variety of reasons. Disturbance is often the main cause, and this is more likely to arise in a mixed aviary, where other species may interfere with the activities of the breeding pair.

Depending on the age of the chicks, you might be able to rear them by hand. But often, if the disturbance happens at night, the young birds will be dead by the time you find them the following morning. You will need a temporary brooder, heated to 37.5°C (100°F) for newly hatched chicks. This can be warmed by an ordinary light bulb, with a less harsh blue bulb being used to simulate the effects of darkness. If the chicks appear distressed and restless, lower the temperature slightly and continue to do this as they get older.

Nowadays, it is relatively easy to provide a suitable diet by using one of the complete rearing foods marketed for hand raising parrot chicks. It is well worth buying a packet before the start of the breeding season, just in case. Put the chicks in a clean margarine tub lined with paper towelling. Use a teaspoon, with its edges bent inwards so that it acts like a funnel, to direct the food into the chicks' gaping beaks. Mix fresh food for each feed, and change the lining of the tub at the same time. The chicks will need regular feeding every couple of hours at first, with a slightly longer gap overnight. Always wipe their beaks after feeding, so they do not become malformed by deposits of food. Similarly, keep the feet clean. As the chicks grow, introduce livefood to their diet. Although hand raising is a time consuming task, softbills generally fledge rapidly – by about three weeks of age in many cases – so this will not be such a longterm commitment as rearing a young parrot, for example.

Hand raising young fruit pigeons and doves is much more difficult, however, because of the constituency of crop milk, which contains no carbohydrate. If the eggs are deserted, it is possible to hatch them artificially in an incubator set at 37.5°C (100°F), with a relative humidity reading of about 50%. Because of the difficulty in rearing the chicks during the first week, it is best to transfer the eggs for hatching under a pair of domesticated Barbary Doves (*Streptopelia 'risoria'*). Offer the adults a varied diet in the hope that they will be able to provide adequate crop milk. If you can synchronize the softbill eggs to hatch at the same time as those of the foster parents, this will help to ensure success.

Availability of young softbills
It is always much easier to hand rear a softbill once it is older and nearly feathered. In many countries, young mynah birds – known as gapers – are taken from their nests just before they are due to fledge. This ensures that the birds will be very tame by the time they are feeding independently. Although this trade is criticized, it does provide an income for local people who will, in turn, encourage and protect the nests of mynah birds. When an export ban was placed on young mynahs in India, the locals lost interest in these birds. As a result, populations of mynahs suffered, with adult birds being taken for the cooking pot.

Health care

If you look after your softbills properly, they will be healthy and long lived. The lifespan of each group varies: some hornbills, for example, live for half a century or more, but size is not a good indication of longevity. Sunbirds for example can live for over a decade in the aviary, although in the wild their lifespan tends to be shorter. There are, however, certain diseases to which softbills are prone, and because stress is often a predisposing factor, recently acquired birds are the most likely to fall ill.

Medication
Only a veterinarian can make an accurate diagnosis of a bird's illness. In some instances laboratory tests may be required, often to ascertain the best course of treatment. One antibiotic may be more effective than another against a particular bacterium, so professional guidance is essential, even in countries where antibiotic remedies are freely available in pet stores. It is often better to dose softbills with tablets, even though this entails catching the bird. In this way, you can at least be certain that it has taken the required amount of medication.

Administering antibiotics through the drinking water, on the other hand, tends to be rather unreliable. This is because a normal softbill diet contains a high percentage of water in the form of fruit, and the birds, therefore, do not need to drink very much. Antibiotic solutions taste bitter, so the bird may be reluctant to drink, even if you remove all other water containers. However, this is the only way to treat nectivores, and you will have to remove their nectar for short periods of time in order to encourage them to drink the medicine. The other option is to inject the drug, but this is not really feasible with such small birds. In a crisis, however, your veterinarian may be forced to take this course of action, because an injection will have a more rapid effect in tackling the ailment.

In an emergency, you may want to administer an antibiotic solution directly into the beak. Do this very carefully, so that you do not choke the bird. Otherwise, keep handling to a minimum. Always wash your hands thoroughly after dealing with a sick bird, to minimize the risk of spreading disease to the others.

A sick bird will need to be separated from its companions in order to reduce the likelihood of them becoming infected. This will also give it a better opportunity to recover in a less stressful environment. You can buy special heated hospital cages, but it is better to devise your own system, using a box cage and a low-power infrared lamp. Hang or angle the lamp over one part of the cage. This way, instead of being kept at a constant temperature, the bird can regulate its own heat by moving nearer to or further away from the lamp. As a guide, the temperature in the warmest part of the cage should be about 27°C (81°F). It is important to leave food and water within easy reach.

Enteric disease
Softbills are perhaps most at risk from enteric disorders, which are spread when their environmental conditions are poor. It is almost impossible to identify the bacteria

Below: *An infrared lamp provides additional heating for a pair of Red-headed Tits. Warmth is vital if ailing birds are to recover.*

involved without laboratory tests. These will also tell you which antibiotic is most effective.

Salmonellosis, which can be introduced to the aviary by rodents, often results in bloodstained diarrhoea, and the subsequent dehydration is fatal. *Salmonella* bacteria are widely distributed and there is a slight risk in feeding the birds raw offal since meat, especially poultry, is often contaminated. These bacteria are destroyed by cooking, and prepared foods such as canned cat food are therefore preferred by some softbill keepers.

Treatment of salmonellosis in small softbills is difficult, since they rapidly become dehydrated. For larger birds, a veterinarian may be able to supplement the fluid lost in the droppings. There is always a slight risk that salmonellosis might be transferred to people in close contact with affected birds, but good hygiene will eliminate this possibility.

The reverse can happen with the bacterium *Escherichia coli*, which owners can pass on to their birds. This micro-organism can also cause enteritis (inflammation of the gut) and may prove fatal. While *E. coli* is a common inhabitant of the mammalian intestinal tract, it is usually harmful to birds. Therefore, you must be careful to wash your hands before cleaning dishes and preparing food for the stock. Newly acquired birds are the most susceptible to such infections, particularly if their diet is altered.

Apart from general signs of illness, it is not unusual for softbills affected with *E. coli* to lose the ability to perch, although their appetites may remain almost normal. Rapid antibiotic treatment can bring about a dramatic reversal of their condition, and a full recovery can be anticipated. As always, complete the course of antibiotics in order to eliminate the bacteria, so that they will not flare up again at a later date. Afterwards, it is a good idea to mix natural yoghourt with the bird's normal food, such as mealworms, for example. Yoghourt contains *Lactobacillus* bacteria, which help to repopulate the gut after a course of antibiotics.

Not all cases of diarrhoea and enteric disease result from bacterial infections. Unicellular organisms – known as protozoa – can give rise to similar symptoms in softbills. The effects tend to be less acute than they would be with a bacterial complaint, and the illness is often referred to as coccidiosis. Certain drugs which act against bacteria may also be effective in these cases, but treatment must depend on the veterinarian's diagnosis. The protozoa can usually be identified by microscopic examination of the bird's droppings.

Botulism
This is a bacterial disease caused by *Clostridium botulinum*, but it is the toxin produced by the bacteria which causes the symptoms. It attacks the nervous system, leading to paralysis, and affected birds are unable to perch. You can differentiate this disease from *E. coli* infections by looking at the legs, which will extend back almost parallel with the tail. The neck too, is often held straight, giving the disease its common name of 'limberneck'.

Botulism is not a common affliction, and unclean maggots are the main source of infection. The putrid meat in the maggots' intestinal tract can be a breeding ground for the clostridial bacteria and, because of this risk, some softbill keepers refuse to give maggots as livefood. Thorough cleaning of the maggots is therefore absolutely essential (see pages 45-46), particularly since an outbreak of botulism may affect all your birds.

Death usually results from respiratory paralysis, and losses can be very high. The only hope of treatment entails the very rapid administration of a specific antitoxin. Those birds at risk, but showing no signs of clinical disease, should be treated immediately with a solution of Epsom salts (hydrated magnesium sulphate). This will act as a purgative, lessening the likelihood of a fatal dose of the toxin being absorbed into the body. Mild cases may recover spontaneously, but you may have to feed the birds a semi-fluid diet – by passing a tube into the crop – until they recover sufficiently to feed alone.

Pseudotuberculosis

This disease – also known as yersiniosis – is another that rodents can spread to aviary birds. Its effects are quite variable, which tends to hamper diagnosis. It is more common during the autumn and winter months, especially when the weather is damp and fairly mild. Certain species, such as toucans, will die very rapidly from pseudotuberculosis, showing few, if any, prior symptoms. Other birds tend to fade away over the course of several days, often with weight loss, leading to 'going light' (see page 13).

The disease can be confirmed by an autopsy; the characteristic markings on the liver resemble those of tuberculosis. Indeed, it is well worth having a post-mortem done on any bird that dies in order to establish the cause of death. You will then be able to take appropriate measures to protect the other birds, including disinfection of the quarters.

Antibiotics can arrest the decline of a bird with pseudotuberculosis, but a full recovery is rare, possibly because of the resultant liver damage. Even after treatment, birds often fail to put on weight, and they tend to remain rather depressed for the remainder of their lives. Pseudotuberculosis is more often encountered in aviaries with earth floors, and you may have to remove the top layer of soil in order to control the infection.

Fungal diseases

Although aspergillosis usually develops quite slowly, it is invariably fatal. Accurate diagnosis while the bird is alive can prove difficult, and although some success has been achieved with the drug ketoconazole, this treatment is unlikely to be worthwhile in most cases.

The effects of this fungus are insidious. Typically, a bird suffering from aspergillosis will look rather depressed. It will be less active than its companions, and its wings may hang down slightly, contributing to its dejected appearance. The fungus usually develops in the air passages, at least in the early stages of the disease. Therefore affected birds may have difficulty in breathing, particularly after a period of exertion. Indeed, catching and handling a softbill suffering from aspergillosis can prove fatal for the bird. Stress of any kind will exacerbate the disease, and towards the end an affected softbill tends to show weight loss over the breastbone.

If an autopsy confirms aspergillosis, clean the bird's quarters very thoroughly, since fungal spores are resilient and will survive in the environment. A solution of caustic soda (sodium hydroxide), although unpleasant to use, will destroy spores in the aviary, but you will also have to check the environmental conditions. Birds housed indoors in humid and badly ventilated quarters are most likely to succumb to this disease. They are particularly at risk if hay is used for nesting purposes, since this is often heavily contaminated with fungal spores.

The prognosis for cases of candidiasis – a fungal infection of the mouth and upper digestive tract – tends to be more favourable, provided that the bird continues feeding. This is particularly important with the smaller nectivores. Apart from treating the disease with an antibiotic prescribed by your veterinarian, it can also be helpful to raise the Vitamin A level in the diet, by adding a tonic to the nectar mixture, for example. Birds afflicted with candidiasis are liable to be deficient in this vitamin, which is stored in the liver. Although long-term overdosing would undoubtedly be harmful, a high dose taken for a week or so will help to overcome this disease considerably, and should have no side effects. (See also page 14 for the telltale signs of candidiasis.)

Parasites
The connection between protozoa and enteric disease has already been mentioned. Other similar organisms can sometimes be found in the bird's blood, but their significance is unclear.

Intestinal worms, on the other hand, certainly do have an adverse effect on a bird's health, contributing to weight loss and debility. Specific remedies for roundworms or tapeworms can be obtained from your veterinarian. All softbills are at risk from roundworms, but, generally, tapeworms tend to affect only the insectivorous species. This is because the insects they eat play an important part in the life cycle of the tapeworm, passing the eggs

Below: *An Orange-bellied Fruitsucker with heavily scaled legs, often a sign of age. Softbills may suffer foot problems.*

from one bird to another. When a bird harbouring the parasite passes the worm eggs in its droppings, these may be eaten by an insect. Only when this insect is itself eaten by another bird will the tapeworm be able to develop to maturity. Roundworms, by comparison, are usually spread directly from bird to bird, without the need for an intermediate host.

Poor feathering in softbills can be attributed to a variety of external parasites, notably mites and lice. These may cause irritation as well as damage to the plumage. Treatment is straightforward, and comes in the form of aerosol sprays. Be sure to use a spray specifically produced for the parasite affecting your bird. Carry out the treatment as a matter of routine when you acquire a new bird, and repeat it about a fortnight later, before you move the bird to its permanent quarters.

Most ectoparasites do not survive well away from the bird's body, but red mites are an exception. These parasites feed on the bird's blood and can cause anaemia. They are liable to establish themselves in the bird's quarters, so treatment of the birds alone will not be sufficient to eliminate these particular parasites. You will need to wash out all cracks and crevices in the bird's quarters with a preparation that kills red mites. Alternatively, you can keep spraying around any holes, with the same aerosol used for the birds. Repeat this procedure, so that you eliminate any mites that may have survived the first treatment. Clearly, because it is extremely troublesome to eliminate these parasites, be sure to take every precaution before releasing new birds into the aviary.

Some softbill keepers advocate using nests discarded by wild birds to encourage breeding. However, this is not recommended, because such nests are often contaminated with red mites which remain dormant until the nest is re-occupied.

Species section

The species featured in this section of the book represent those softbills which are usually available to birdkeepers, and include representatives of all the major groupings. The birds are introduced under family headings, such as hummingbirds, sunbirds, tanagers, bulbuls and starlings. Other species are included, but not necessarily introduced with appropriate headings. Softbills vary quite widely in their requirements, so consider carefully the individual needs of the species that interests you before acquiring any birds. Omnivorous softbills are the easiest birds to maintain, and often prove the most reliable to breed.

Softbills are popular exhibition subjects. The condition of the birds is of paramount importance for judging purposes; as well as the feathering, the bird's feet and toes must be unblemished. Softbills that lack claws are unlikely to take top honours at any event. If possible, exhibit only aviary-bred stock, since such birds

are invariably tamer and less nervous in the confines of a show cage. Steadiness, which is usually a reflection of the time spent in training the bird, is an important factor during judging, because a bird that refuses to perch will not be seen to best effect.

You may enter either one softbill or a pair together. Generally speaking, cocks are preferred as single exhibition subjects, since they are usually more colourful and likely to create a better impression on the judge. If a pair is exhibited, both birds must be in top condition and, since this is harder to achieve, a pair will invariably beat a single bird of equal quality.

Never enter a softbill in a large number of shows. To begin with, minimize travelling by concentrating on perhaps one or two shows in your neighbourhood. Once you have been successful locally, you may want to venture further afield and enter one of the larger regional shows.

Hummingbirds are confined to the Americas, where more than 300 are known to exist and new species are still being discovered. In spite of their frail appearance, hummingbirds can prove quite hardy and some species migrate over considerable distances. One of the more northerly species, the Rufous Hummingbird (*Selasphorus rufous*), flies nearly 6000 kilometres (3750 miles) back and forth from Mexico to as far north as Alaska, where it breeds during the summer. The largest member of the family Trochilidae is found in the Southern Hemisphere, occurring in the Andean region south to Chile. The Giant Hummingbird (*Patagona gigas*) is about 20cm (8in) in overall size, contrasting with the aptly named Bee Hummingbird (*Mellisuga helenae*), which is the smallest known species, barely 6cm (2.4in) in length.

Violet-bellied Hummingbird

Damophila julie
● **Distribution:** Panama, to northern Ecuador.
● **Size:** 10cm (4in).
● **Diet:** Nectar solution and small insects, notably fruit flies.
● **Sexing:** Hens are significantly duller, having greyish white underparts.
● **Compatibility:** Not too aggressive, and may even be intimidated by other hummingbirds in a communal flight.

These hummingbirds are an attractive species and make an ideal introduction to this group of nectivores. Cocks will sing quite readily, which adds to their charm. Bathing facilities are essential and the Violet-bellied will readily enter a shallow saucer of water provided for this purpose. When displaying, the cock perches close to his intended mate, flapping his wings and singing loudly. However, if the cock appears to persecute the hen, it is advisable to separate the birds for a period.

Some species of hummingbird are more aggressive than others. Under these circumstances, the sexes may need to be kept apart for much of the time. However, when a hen shows signs of nest building, introduce a cock bird for short periods, ideally through a partition of some kind. Remove the cock permanently once egg laying has started, otherwise he may interfere with the hen's breeding and rearing activities.

The Violet-bellied Hummingbird does not appear to have been bred successfully in any collection at present, but other species have nested and reared chicks. The hen alone incubates the eggs for about a fortnight, before the chicks hatch. Free access to fruit flies is vital during the rearing period.

Fledging occurs when the young hummingbirds are about four weeks old, but at this stage they are much duller than adults, lacking their distinctive iridescence. Within a week, the chicks will feed independently. At this time they should be removed to separate quarters, as the hen is likely to attack them from this stage onwards. These hummingbirds can live for seven years or more under favourable conditions in captivity.

Below:
Violet-bellied Hummingbird
These small birds are often very aggressive towards each other.

Above: **Rufous-vented Whitetip Hummingbird**
Many hummingbirds become tame, showing no fear in captivity.

Rufous-vented Whitetip Hummingbird

Urosticte ruficrissa
● **Distribution:** Western Colombia and Ecuador, extending into northeastern Peru.
● **Size:** 12.5cm (5in).
● **Diet:** Nectar solution and small insects, especially fruit flies.
● **Sexing:** Hens have white underparts speckled with green.
● **Compatibility:** Cocks in particular may prove aggressive.

This species is sometimes grouped with the Green-vented Whitetip (*U. benjamini*) as a subspecies. Although females are very similar in appearance, male Rufous-vented Whitetips lack the prominent area of purple plumage present on the breast of their close relative, and have buff, rather than green, undertail coverts. They frequently become very tame, and settle well in a spacious flight.

Before you buy these birds, always check the skin over the breastbone, as this is a common site for injury, but if the wound is not severe the hummingbird should recover uneventfully. Keep this species in a temperature range of 18-20°C (64-68°F) since the birds will develop signs of heat

stress if the temperature reaches 30°C (86°F). A minimum of twelve hours of daylight is recommended to give the birds adequate opportunity to feed, otherwise their condition is likely to decline progressively. They will often bathe quite readily, so provide a shallow saucer of water, changed daily.

When hummingbirds roost overnight, signs of torpor may be apparent. They cling to the perch, seemingly motionless, but will come to life at daybreak. If a hummingbird becomes torpid during the day, it may be because it is housed at too low a temperature. Alternatively, it could be unwell, or have run out of food. It is advisable to provide at least two nectar tubes, so that a reserve is available if you are absent for most of the day just in case the solution leaks out of one bottle. If hummingbirds are housed together, a choice of feeding sites is essential, since one individual may monopolize a single feeder.

If you decide to keep hummingbirds, you must appreciate that they are especially demanding aviary occupants. They are unsuitable for small flight cages, where they rapidly become overweight. They cannot be recommended for the novice softbill enthusiast but, in experienced hands, they should prove quite long-lived. Certainly, more are now being bred.

SUNBIRDS

While the sunbirds bear a superficial resemblance to hummingbirds, they do not possess the ability to hover. Like hummingbirds, they are extremely nimble in flight, darting in and out among flowers seeking nectar and insects. There are just over 100 species of sunbird, occurring throughout much of the Old World, from Africa and neighbouring offshore islands across Asia.

Sunbirds range in overall size from about 10cm (4in) to 23cm (9in). Some species are long tailed. Cock birds are invariably more brightly coloured than hens, so sexing is straightforward in most species. Notable exceptions are the so-called spiderhunters of the genus *Arachnothera*, where both sexes are predominantly greenish in colour.

Lesser Double-collared Sunbird

Nectarinia chalybea
● **Distribution:** Southern Africa.
● **Size:** 12.5cm (5in).
● **Diet:** A nectar solution, small insects such as fruit flies, finely diced fruit and a fine-grade insectivorous food.
● **Sexing:** Cock birds are metallic green with narrow collars of metallic blue and metallic red plumage under the throat. Hens are greyish olive overall. Young birds resemble hens.
● **Compatibility:** Pairs are best kept apart from each other in aviaries.

Below:
Lesser Double-collared Sunbird
The male, shown here, is usually more colourful than the female.

Various forms of the Double-collared Sunbird occur throughout Africa, differing in both size and the extent of red coloration on the

breast. This species has a relatively short bill compared with the Greater form, (*N. afra*) and tends to be found at lower altitudes. Like other sunbirds, they are susceptible to candidiasis, and their nectar bottles must be kept spotlessly clean to prevent the spread of this disease (see page 00). Low levels of Vitamin A can predispose birds to infection and a multivitamin powder sprinkled over the food or dissolved in the drinking water is extremely beneficial, particularly for newly acquired sunbirds. They should then settle in without problems.

Malachite Sunbird

Nectarinia famosa

● **Distribution:** East Africa from southern Sudan south to Cape Province, in upland areas.

● **Size:** Cocks with their long tails may be 23cm (9in) overall. Body size is about 12.5cm (5in).

● **Diet:** Nectar, small insects, finely diced fruit and fine-grade softbill food.

● **Sexing:** Cocks are easily distinguished by their green rump and wing coverts, even when in eclipse plumage (i.e. the relatively dull plumage of cock birds outside the breeding season). Young birds resemble adult hens, but are darker with a shorter beak.

● **Compatibility:** Cocks should not be mixed with related species.

This striking species tends to be found at altitudes above 1525m (5000ft) in areas of moorland and scrub. It is thus one of the hardiest sunbirds. Cocks moult into their colourful breeding plumage at the onset of the breeding period. For the rest of the year they are brownish grey, but retain their long tails. They can be distinguished from the closely related but slightly larger Scarlet-tufted Malachite Sunbird (*N. johnstoni*) by the bright yellow plumage in the pectoral region at the top of the wings.

Malachite Sunbirds have been bred successfully in captivity. The first breeding record appears to date back to 1964, when a pair nested in a small outdoor aviary measuring approximately 1.8x0.9m (6x3ft). The hen built her nest in a clump of bamboo, using grass, feathers and even string in its construction. She laid a single egg, which hatched after about 13 days. The chick was reared on fruit flies and aphids and left the nest when just over a fortnight old. It was seen drinking nectar at the age of 19 days and catching fruit flies soon afterwards.

Left: **Malachite Sunbirds**
It is easy to distinguish the cock bird (left) at breeding time, when he undergoes a seasonal moult.

Variable Sunbird

Nectarinia venusta
● **Distribution:** Occurs over much of East and Central Africa.
● **Size:** 10cm (4in).
● **Diet:** A nectar solution, finely diced fruit and fine-grade insectivorous food, as well as insects, such as fruit flies, given daily.
● **Sexing:** Cocks have a bluish green head and purplish throat and chest. Hens are olive-grey with a yellowish white belly. Young birds resemble adult hens in their colour pattern.
● **Compatibility:** Pairs should be kept apart from each other, and from related species.

Various local races of this sunbird occur over its wide distribution. Cock birds remain in colour throughout the year. Individuals tend to differ quite noticeably in appearance, as the name of the species indicates. Belly coloration

Above: **Variable Sunbird**
Although they will take other foods, sunbirds must have access to a nectar solution at all times. This is a splendid cock bird.

can vary from orange through yellow to a pale lemon-white. Field studies suggest a natural surplus of cock birds in the wild and, indeed, hens may be difficult to acquire. Accurate identification of hen sunbirds often requires reference to a specialist field guide, because many species tend to be so similar in appearance.

Variable Sunbirds may occasionally construct nests which are domed, rather than suspended from a branch like those of most sunbird species. When displaying, the cock birds clearly exhibit their yellow-orange pectoral tufts. Two darkly speckled eggs form the usual clutch. They hatch after about a fortnight, and the chicks fledge about a fortnight later.

Grey-breasted Spiderhunter
Arachnothera affinis
● **Distribution:** Southeast Asia, from the Malay Peninsula and southern Burma to Borneo, Sumatra, Java and neighbouring islands.
● **Size:** 18cm (7in).
● **Diet:** Nectar, diced fruit mixed with a fine-grade insectivorous food and a daily supply of insects.
● **Sexing:** No visual distinctions between the sexes. Young birds lack the streaking present on the underparts of adults.
● **Compatibility:** Tend not to be aggressive, even towards smaller hummingbirds.

Although they lack the bright coloration of many Asian sunbirds, the closely related spiderhunters can be fascinating aviary occupants. As their name suggests, they will readily take spiders and similar livefood, and tend to be less dependent on nectar than sunbirds. Spider-hunters may be reluctant to sample other items, such as finely diced fruit, but if they are housed with species such as Zosterops, they should soon start to take a varied diet quite readily. Although breeding attempts have been made in aviary surroundings, it appears that no chicks have been successfully reared to date.

Spiderhunters are reasonably hardy once acclimatized. However, like sunbirds, they need to be kept in heated indoor accommodation throughout the winter in temperate climates. If provided with a shallow dish of water, they will bathe quite readily under these conditions.

Below:
Grey-breasted Spiderhunter
Spiderhunters are closely related to sunbirds, but generally duller.

Red-legged Honeycreeper

Cyanerpes cyaneus

● **Distribution:** Mexico, south to Panama, also over most of South America as far south as Brazil.

● **Size:** 10cm (4in).

● **Diet:** Nectar solution, finely diced fruit covered with softbill food and suitable soft-bodied livefood.

● **Sexing:** Cock birds in colour are a striking combination of blue and black, with yellow evident on the underside of their flight feathers. Out of breeding colour (i.e. in eclipse plumage), they resemble hens, but their legs are a darker shade of red.

● **Compatibility:** Tend not to be aggressive and can be housed with other nectivores of similar disposition, such as Zosterops.

Honeycreepers are closely related to the tanagers. They are also known as sugar birds, and this particular species is sometimes called the Yellow-winged Sugar Bird. Sugar birds often attempt to

Above:
Red-legged Honeycreeper
These nectivores, also known as sugar birds, are not difficult to keep. Pairs often breed readily.

nest in aviary surroundings. A variety of materials will be taken to construct the nest, typically cup-shaped, which is hidden in vegetation. Two eggs form the usual clutch, and the incubation period is about a fortnight. Plenty of livefood is essential for rearing the chicks, and moths caught in an insect trap have been used successfully for this purpose. A rearing food may also be given at this time. The young sugar birds should leave the nest within about three weeks. Young cocks resemble hens when they leave the nest, and will first show signs of their brilliant purple coloration on the head. Warm winter housing is necessary, although in fairly mild localities they can be kept in an outside aviary through the summer. The related Purple Sugar Bird (*C. caeruleus*) does not show eclipse plumage.

Bananaquit
Coereba flaveola
● **Distribution:** Over much of Central and South America, extending to the Caribbean.
● **Size:** 10cm (4in).
● **Diet:** Nectar solution, finely diced fruit covered with softbill food, plus suitable soft-bodied livefood.
● **Sexing:** Hens are usually paler on their underparts than cocks and young birds have a yellow tinge to their eye stripe. There is considerable regional variation, with up to 35 races being identified.
● **Compatibility:** Can be a nuisance in an aviary containing breeding pairs of other species, but will live together in a group.

These lively, active birds are naturally quite tame. They are relatively simple to cater for, although they are not hardy. When breeding, the cock is primarily responsible for nest construction. The hen adds the finishing touches, usually feathers for lining the structure. Clutch size varies from two to six eggs, which are greyish and speckled with brown markings. The hen tends to sit alone and the eggs should hatch within about 12 days. Livefood is vital during the rearing period. The chicks should fledge after a further 18 days and will be independent within a further fortnight. In spite of their name, Bananaquits rarely show any preference for this fruit; caterpillars and spiders are often favourite livefoods.

Below: **Bananaquit**
These lively softbills occur across a wide geographical range. Some forms are much more colourful than others. Often become tame.

TANAGERS

The tanagers, another New World group, comprise over 200 species, occurring in a wide range of localities. The *Tangara* tanagers are the most common in avicultural circles, but members of other genera are also sometimes available. These include the *Ramphocelus* species, which are primarily reddish in colour. Colour feeding is likely to be required with such tanagers to maintain their appearance over successive moults.

Black-eared Golden Tanager

Tangara arthus
● **Distribution:** North and eastern parts of South America.
● **Size:** 12.5cm (5in).
● **Diet:** Fruit, mynah pellets and insectivorous food. Some livefood and possibly nectar, especially for recently imported individuals.
● **Sexing:** Hens may be paler overall, while young birds are duller than their parents.
● **Compatibility:** Can occasionally prove aggressive.

This species, one of the more commonly seen *Tangara* tanagers, has been bred successfully in aviaries on various occasions. Pairs may nest repeatedly if kept in a planted enclosure and provided with adequate livefood for rearing purposes. In common with other members of the genus, the clutch usually consists of only two eggs. The incubation period is 14 days and the young birds should leave the nest after a similar interval.

These attractive tanagers can prove quite long-lived birds, and may thrive well into their teens.

Below:
Black-eared Golden Tanager
Sexing these lively and long-lived tanagers visually is very difficult.

Above: **Palm Tanager**
Although not as colourful as some species, these larger tanagers are relatively hardy once acclimatized.

Palm Tanager

Thraupis palmarum
● **Distribution:** Extends from Central America southwards, occurring east of the Andes.
● **Size:** 18cm (7in).
● **Diet:** Diced fruit, covered with softbill food and mixed with mynah pellets if available. Livefood is also required.
● **Sexing:** No reliable visual distinction possible; hens may be slightly paler.
● **Compatibility:** Liable to be aggressive, certainly to smaller species.

Although lacking the bright coloration associated with the *Tangara* species, members of the genus *Thraupis* have attractive pastel shades in their plumage. They also tend to be hardier, and in mild areas it may be possible to keep them in an outside aviary without artificial heat throughout the year, once they are acclimatized. Breeding details are similar to those of the previous species. Other relatively hardy tanagers include the Mountain Tanagers, belonging to the genera *Buthraupis* and *Anisognathus*. They require similar care.

75

Bay-headed Tanager
Tangara gyrola
● **Distribution:** From Costa Rica and Panama, extending across much of South America to Ecuador, Bolivia and Brazil.
● **Size:** 12.5cm (5in).
● **Diet:** Fruit, mynah pellets and insectivorous food. Some livefood and possibly nectar, especially for recently imported individuals.
● **Sexing:** Hens may be slightly duller in overall coloration, but this distinction is not entirely reliable.
● **Compatibility:** May occasionally prove aggressive, but generally amenable towards softbills of similar size.

These tanagers are popular avicultural subjects. They occur over a wide area and up to nine subspecies are recognized, differing in various respects from each other. You cannot rely on plumage distinctions as a means of sexing these birds. Young Bay-headed Tanagers are predominantly green overall, lacking the bluish underparts and the characteristic coloration of the head. Breeding details correspond to those of the related Black-eared Golden Tanager.

Euphonias and chlorophonias

Above: **Bay-headed Tanager**
Do not rely on variations in the depth of head coloration as a means of sexing these tanagers.

are two related groups of birds with similar habits to the tanagers. They tend to be frugivorous in their feeding habits and are often particularly fond of berries of various kinds. Euphonias are likely to attempt to breed in planted surroundings, constructing a domed-shaped nest rather than the cup-shaped nest typical of the tanagers. Breeding details are similar, however, but since it can be difficult to differentiate between euphonia hens of various species, a supposed pair may actually produce hybrid offspring.

Chlorophonias are similar to euphonias, being about 10cm (4in) in size. It is easy to sex them, since the hens are duller overall. In the wild, they are found at higher altitudes and can be more difficult to establish in an aviary as a result. However, once acclimatized, they prove quite hardy, but do not overwinter them unless you can provide artificial heating. Chlorophonias tend to be less destructive towards plants in their enclosure than euphonias.

White-eye
Zosterops palpebrosa
● **Distribution:** The Indian sub-continent, eastwards to China.
● **Size:** 11.5cm (4.5in).
● **Diet:** Fine softbill food, diced fruit, small insects and nectar.
● **Sexing:** No visual distinction possible between the sexes.
● **Compatibility:** Compatible in groups and with other small birds.

Zosterops as a group have a wide distribution, occurring across much of Africa to Australasia. They are adaptable birds and are easy to maintain in aviaries. However, accurate identification is not always straightforward, for more than 80 species and numerous subspecies are recognized. There are, in fact, 12 races of *Zosterops palpebrosa* alone. Another of the Asiatic White-eyes often available is the distinctive Chestnut-flanked (*Z. erythropleura*), with brown markings on the side of its body. The African Zosterops tend to be more yellow in overall coloration, but some variation again can be anticipated: indeed, 20 subspecies of the Yellow White-eye (*Z. senegalensis*) have been identified.

The cock's song is heard only during the breeding period. A small cup-shaped nest is built, often incorporating spiders' webs if available, and up to four eggs may be laid within. These hatch after an incubation period of 12 days. A constant supply of soft-bodied livefood is vital for successful rearing of the chicks, which fledge when about a fortnight old.

Zosterops are not hardy and should be kept in heated surroundings over the winter in temperate climates. They are fond of sponge cake soaked in nectar, but you should never provide nectar in open containers, since the birds may attempt to bathe in the solution, with catastrophic results. This warning also applies to other softbills.

Below: **White-eye or Zosterops**
Zosterops are adaptable and easy to keep. An ideal introduction to the nectivorous softbills in general.

BARBETS

Barbets have a wide distribution, occurring in South America as well as Africa and Asia. Their name is derived from the barb-like bristles around the base of their stout and powerful beaks. The dietary needs of these birds vary quite widely: the African species, found in scrubland, tend to be basically insectivorous, whereas New World barbets appear to be primarily frugivorous in their feeding habits.

Pied Barbet

Tricholaema leucomelan
● **Distribution:** Southern Africa to Angola and Zambia.
● **Size:** 15cm (6in).
● **Diet:** Softbill food, including mynah pellets, fruit and insects.
● **Sexing:** No visual distinction possible between the sexes.
● **Compatibility:** Likely to prove aggressive.

These small barbets are lively and, once a pair is identified, are best kept in an aviary on their own. Provide them with a nestbox for roosting and breeding, disguising the entrance with cork bark if necessary. Pied Barbets have bred successfully in aviaries, with up to three eggs forming the usual clutch. The incubation period is 14 days and the young birds should fledge about 21 days later. At this stage, they have not yet developed the serrations ('teeth') on the sides of the beak, or the characteristic area of red plumage on the head.

Fire-tufted Barbet

Psilopogon pyrolophus
● **Distribution:** Malaysia and Sumatra.
● **Size:** 25cm (10in).
● **Diet:** Softbill food, including mynah pellets, fruit and insects.
● **Sexing:** No visual distinction possible between the sexes.
● **Compatibility:** Liable to prove aggressive.

These striking Asiatic barbets are more frugivorous in their feeding habits than the previous species. Unfortunately, there is no reliable method of sexing, although some distinctions, such as variation in eye coloration, have been suggested. Thus, pairs can only be recognized by surgical sexing. They need to be housed on their own, preferably in a flight planted with dense and tough vegetation. This provides cover for the hen. Cocks may become very savage at the onset of the breeding season, and it may even be necessary to separate the birds for a time. Careful supervision will be required to ensure breeding success.

Below: **Pied Barbet**
Barbets are easily distinguished by the 'bristles' at the base of their beaks. Provide suitable logs on which the birds can exercise their powerful beaks, rather than attack the aviary framework. They may live for at least ten years.

Above: **Flame-headed Barbet**
This species is easy to sex by its head coloration. Provide generous amounts of fruit for these barbets.

Flame-headed Barbet

Eubucco bourcierii
● **Distribution:** Central America, from Costa Rica to Panama, and the Andean region of Colombia and Ecuador.
● **Size:** 18cm (7in).
● **Diet:** Softbill food, including mynah pellets, fruit and livefood.
● **Sexing:** Only cocks have bright red heads: those of hens are greyish.
● **Compatibility:** Keep pairs apart.

Although New World barbets tend to be quite scarce in aviculture, this species may be occasionally encountered. Like barbets from other parts of the world, these birds are not hardy and must be kept in frost-free accommodation throughout the winter. You must equip their quarters with wood, which they can attack with their powerful beaks. Silver birch logs are often favoured for this purpose, but ensure that these show no signs of fungus. The destructive capabilities of barbets are quite surprising: some species may even tunnel into the floor of their aviary. Their calls are sometimes quite loud, but those of the species listed here should not cause undue offence.

Below: **Fire-tufted Barbet**
Another highly frugivorous species. These barbets inhabit mountainous forests in Southeast Asia. Although quite large, this is not the biggest barbet. The Giant Barbet, Megalaima virens, *found in parts of the Himalayas through to southern China, grows to 30cm (12in). Both species can become aggressive.*

Red-billed Toucan
Ramphastos tucanus
● **Distribution:** From southeast Venezuela and the Guianas extending to northern Brazil.
● **Size:** 45cm (18in).
● **Diet:** Mynah pellets, diced fruit sprinkled with insectivorous food and livefood of suitable size, such as mealworms.
● **Sexing:** No clear visual distinction between the sexes, but hens may have smaller beaks.

Left: **Red-billed Toucan**
The elaborate and colourful bills of these birds are very light, with an inner honeycombed construction.

● **Compatibility:** Best kept in individual pairs. Will even kill smaller birds.

The *Ramphastos* toucans, including the well-known Toco Toucan (*R. toco*), are the most common in aviculture. In some cases it is possible to sex them by variations in bill size and shape, but this is not entirely reliable. Surgical sexing has greatly facilitated the breeding of toucans in aviary surroundings. Palm logs with hollow centres are often favoured as breeding sites, otherwise fairly deep nestboxes should be provided. Two or three white eggs form the usual clutch and hatch quite rapidly, usually within 19 days of laying. The chicks have relatively small beaks. They develop quite slowly, not opening their eyes until they are three weeks old and finally fledging approximately seven weeks after hatching. At this stage, they are duller than their parents, with smaller beaks. Adult birds will readily take young mice and similar items of livefood when they have chicks in the nest.

Scarlet-rumped Aracari
Pteroglossus erythropygius
● **Distribution:** Western Ecuador.
● **Size:** 40cm (16in).
● **Diet:** Mynah pellets, diced fruit sprinkled with insectivorous food, and livefood of suitable size, such as mealworms.
● **Sexing:** No visual distinction between the sexes.
● **Compatibility:** May agree in small groups, but pairs should be kept apart.

Also known as the Pale-mandibled Aracari, this species may be confused at first glance with the Banded or Collared Aracari from Central America. Yet study of the

Left: **Toco Toucan**
This species – the largest and most spectacular member of the family – was known in Europe as long ago as 1527. Within the beak runs a long, fringed tongue.

beaks will serve to distinguish these aracaris. In the case of the Pale-mandibled, black markings are confined to a thin streak along the upper part of the beak and at the tip of the lower mandible.

Aracaris tend to be less popular than the *Ramphastos* species, but they make fascinating aviary occupants. Their calls, unlike those of their larger relatives, are not disturbing. Once acclimatized, they can be quite hardy, but they must be given adequate protection, particularly against frost. Indeed, the plumage of all toucans is quite thin, providing little insulation against cold weather, and in extreme cases their beaks can be damaged by frostbite. Aracaris will often roost in nestboxes and should be encouraged to do so. They are inveterate bathers, even when kept indoors. Give them a clean washing-up bowl partially filled with water for this purpose.

Apart from aracaris, the striking Emerald Toucanets belonging to the genus *Alaucorhynchus* are also occasionally available to

Above:
Red-rumped Green Toucanet
This species is also known as the Chestnut-billed Emerald Toucanet.

Below: **Scarlet-rumped Aracari**
These attractive members of the toucan family are easy to keep.

Above: **Red-billed Hornbill**
The hen bird is sealed into the nesting chamber in the breeding period, and fed there by her mate.

Below: **Yellow-billed Hornbill**
Less common than its Red-billed relative, but needs similar care.

aviculturists. They have been bred successfully, with the use of deep nestboxes. These birds tend to be more nervous than aracaris and rarely become as confiding.

Some care is needed when introducing unfamiliar toucan-like birds; they can prove aggressive, especially a cock in breeding condition. It is advisable to catch the established bird and transfer both back to the aviary together.

Red-billed Hornbill
Tockus erythrorhynchus
● **Distribution:** Occurs over a broad band of Africa, from Senegal to Somalia and Tanzania.
● **Size:** 45cm (18in).
● **Diet:** Mynah pellets, insects, chopped meat and diced fruit.
● **Sexing:** Hens generally have smaller, paler beaks.
● **Compatibility:** Should be housed in individual pairs for breeding purposes.

Most hornbills are too large for the average suburban aviary, but this species and the related Yellow-billed (*T. flavirostris*) are sometimes kept. Although not especially colourful, they are fascinating aviary occupants when breeding. You must provide a mixture of damp mud and clay, which the cock bird will use to seal the hen in the nestbox. Here she will incubate a clutch of six eggs, remaining with the chicks until they are ready to leave the nest at about 10 weeks of age. The cock bird feeds her through a small hole left in the front of the sealed entrance. Invertebrates are vital for the rearing of the chicks and must be given in large quantities.

When the birds are due to emerge, check that the clay has not set so hard as to prevent the hornbills from breaking out. Remove the young birds as soon as they are feeding themselves; otherwise they may be attacked by their parents, who may wish to nest again. These hornbills are hardy in captivity once fully acclimatized, but they are particularly susceptible to frostbite.

BULBULS

This family of more than 120 species, with representatives both in Africa and Asia. Bulbuls are not especially colourful birds, although they may become quite talented songsters. They are not difficult to cater for in aviary surroundings and are generally keen to breed.

Red-vented Bulbul

Pycnonotus cafer
● **Distribution:** India, extending to much of Southeast Asia.
● **Size:** 23cm (9in).
● **Diet:** Diced fruit, softbill food and mynah pellets, plus livefood.
● **Sexing:** No visual distinction possible between the sexes.
● **Compatibility:** Not usually aggressive.

Bulbuls will frequently attempt to breed when housed in a planted aviary. Both sexes help to construct the nest, which is usually well hidden by vegetation. The eggs are pinkish white in colour, with darker blotches; three form the usual clutch. Incubation, during which the hen sits alone, may not start until the clutch is complete. The chicks should hatch after about 13 days. Fledging should occur after a similar period. At this stage, the young bulbuls have whitish edges to the bill. Provide small soft-bodied livefood for rearing purposes and, once the chicks are independent, remove them to separate accommodation. Meanwhile, the adult birds may begin to nest again.

Yellow-vented Bulbul

Pycnonotus aurigaster
● **Distribution:** A wide area of Southeast Asia, extending to China and certain offshore islands.
● **Size:** 18cm (7in).
● **Diet:** Standard softbill fare, including fruit and livefood.
● **Sexing:** No visual distinction possible between the sexes.
● **Compatibility:** Can be housed with softbills of similar size if desired.

Although some bulbuls can be persuaded to use a canary nesting pan for breeding purposes, they generally prefer to build their own nests. Cock birds sing quite frequently when in breeding condition, and this can provide a means of recognizing pairs. In mild areas it is possible to keep bulbuls in unheated outdoor accommodation throughout the year, once they are acclimatized. Their plumage is quite fine, however, and so bring them indoors if they show signs of discomfort during cold weather.

Below: **Red-eared Bulbul**
One of the most common, but less colourful, species. They have an attractive prominent crest.

Above: **Yellow-vented Bulbul**
This and other Asiatic species are the bulbuls most frequently available to birdkeepers.

Left: **Red-vented Bulbul**
Once fully acclimatized, and given access to inside accommodation, bulbuls are usually quite hardy.

Red-eared Bulbul
Pynonotus jocosus
● **Distribution:** India across Southeast Asia into China.
● **Size:** 18cm (7in).
● **Diet:** Softbill food, fruit and livefood.
● **Sexing:** No visual distinction possible between the sexes.
● **Compatibility:** Quite tolerant, but pairs are best kept apart.

Like other bulbuls, the Red-eared, with its attractive and prominent crest, is quite easy to establish. They can become quite tame and will settle well in aviary surroundings. Other Asian bulbuls that are sometimes available include the Collared Finchbill (*Spizixos semitorques*), which will take small seeds in addition to the usual range of softbill foods.
The African species are far less commonly seen in aviaries than those of Asiatic origin.

85

Fairy Bluebird

Irena puella

- **Distribution:** India and across much of Southeast Asia.
- **Size:** 25cm (10in).
- **Diet:** Fruit and softbill food, plus invertebrates of suitable size.
- **Sexing:** Cocks have glossy blue plumage on their backs and black elsewhere; hens are dark blue.
- **Compatibility:** May prove aggressive, so keep pairs on their own.

These birds are striking aviary occupants but can be difficult to establish. During this period, they will benefit from being offered a wide range of foodstuffs, even a nectar solution. They need planted surroundings to encourage breeding activity, since the nest is usually built in a bush. The clutch of two eggs should hatch after 13 days. If all goes well, fledging occurs after a similar period. Chicks of both sexes resemble adult hens, but have dark eyes. The adult birds will become highly insectivorous throughout the rearing period. Fairy Bluebirds are prone to foot problems, such as bumblefoot, particularly when kept in indoor flights; in such accommodation be sure to wash or replace their perches frequently.

Above: **Fairy Bluebird**
This is a cock bird. Sexing is straightforward in this species, as hens are significantly duller.

Right: **Golden-fronted Fruitsucker**
An attractive species, but breeding is a problem, since cocks often prove aggressive towards hens.

Golden-fronted Fruitsucker

Chloropsis aurifrons
● **Distribution:** From India to Southeast Asia.
● **Size:** 25cm (10in).
● **Diet:** Softbill food, with fruit and livefood. Nectar can also be supplied.
● **Sexing:** Hens have green foreheads and less black plumage.
● **Compatibility:** Can prove aggressive.

Fruitsuckers are birds of forested areas, where they conceal themselves among vegetation, so you must house them in densely planted enclosures. This should help to prevent a hen being persecuted by her potential mate. It is difficult to obtain compatible pairs: fruitsuckers should be introduced at the same time to a new enclosure, so that neither bird establishes a territorial advantage. Cock birds rank among the most attractive songsters. The breeding habits of fruitsuckers are similar to those of Fairy Bluebirds, with whom they are grouped in the family Irenidae.

Other species are occasionally available, such as Hardwick's Fruitsucker (*Chloropsis hardwickei*), and need similar care.

Orange-headed Ground Thrush

Zoothera citrina
● **Distribution:** From India to Southeast Asia and China.
● **Size:** 20cm (8in).
● **Diet:** Typical softbill diet, with some fruit and invertebrates.
● **Sexing:** Compared with cocks, hens are duller overall with brownish upperparts.
● **Compatibility:** Pairs should be kept apart.

The ground thrushes form a large genus of 29 species, with representatives occurring in Africa as well as Asia. However, with the exception of the Orange-Headed Ground Thrush, they tend to be scarce avicultural subjects. As

Above:
Orange-headed Ground Thrush
This species will spend much of its time on the floor of its quarters.

their name suggests, these birds forage extensively on the floor of their quarters, although they will build their nest above ground level. The melodic song of the cock is most noticeable during the nesting season. A typical clutch consists of four greenish white eggs, marked with brown blotches. Both birds share the incubation, but after hatching, the cock spends most of his time off the nest, returning to feed his brooding mate. The young ground thrushes should leave the nest about two and half weeks after hatching.

Siberian Thrush

Zoothera sibirica

● **Distribution:** Siberia and south to Mongolia and Japan. Moves further southwards during the winter, extending from Southeast Asia into China.

● **Size:** 25cm (10in).

● **Diet:** Typical softbill fare, plus fruit and invertebrates.

● **Sexing:** Cocks are predominantly slate-grey with white stripes above the eyes, whereas hens are brownish overall with barring on their underparts. The hens have prominent buff-coloured streaks above their eyes.

● **Compatibility:** Keep pairs apart from each other.

The Siberian Ground Thrush is similar to the preceding species in its habits, and has become more familiar in aviculture during recent years, although it cannot be described as common. A well-planted aviary will encourage a pair to start nesting. It is safest not to house them alongside other ground-dwelling birds, since cocks can become quite aggressive during the breeding period. Livefood will be essential for the successful rearing of the chicks. Remove the young birds once they are feeding independently, as the adults may have a second clutch of eggs. Siberian Thrushes are reasonably hardy, but are at risk from frostbite. They can also be susceptible to foot ailments, notably bumblefoot, if kept in dirty surroundings.

Below: **Siberian Thrush**
A well-planted aviary provides the best means of housing these fine thrushes; here they may breed.

Snowy-crowned Robin Chat

Cossypha niveicapilla
● **Distribution:** Senegal southwards to northern Angola, and eastwards to western Kenya.
● **Size:** 20cm (8in).
● **Diet:** Softbill food, plus insects and fruit.
● **Sexing:** No visual distinctions possible between the sexes.
● **Compatibility:** Best kept apart from related birds.

The Robin Chat is another member of the thrush family (*Turdidae*) and, like related species, makes its natural home in woodland. Therefore, it does best in a densely planted aviary, where it will often forage for food at ground level. A pair may adopt a nestbox when breeding, building a simple nest within on which to lay the eggs. Two eggs appear to form the usual clutch, and these should hatch after an incubation period of 14 days. The young fledge when they are about 14 days old. The adult

Above:
Snowy-crowned Robin Chat
Various robin chats are sometimes available in captivity – all need similar care. Shy by nature.

birds are likely to prove very shy when breeding, so leave them alone as much as possible. Offer increasing quantities of livefood when the chicks are due to hatch. At this stage, the parents may also take minced meat. When they first leave the nest, the youngsters are duller than their parents.

White-crested Jay Thrush

Garrulax leucolophus
● **Distribution:** From India across Southeast Asia.
● **Size:** 30cm (12in).
● **Diet:** Usual softbill fare, including diced fruit and livefood.
● **Sexing:** Hens may have smaller, greyer crests.
● **Compatibility:** Aggressive. Do not introduce a newcomer to a group. Pairs should be kept apart, otherwise fighting may occur.

Above: **White-crested Jay Thrush**
These striking jay thrushes are hardy once acclimatized, but can prove aggressive when breeding.

Below: **Hoami**
The Hoami, a talented songster, is also known as the Melodious Jay Thrush and Chinese Nightingale.

This species makes a lively aviary occupant and possesses an attractive song. The jay thrushes are another large genus, embracing more than 40 species, with the Hoami (*G. canorus*) being considered the best songster in the group.

The White-crested Jay Thrush is relatively hardy once acclimatized and is omnivorous in its feeding habits. It will readily eat pinkies (day-old mice) and various meats, especially during the breeding period. The birds build a cup-shaped nest in suitable vegetation. The adults share incubation of the eggs, and the chicks hatch after about 13 days. After fledging, move the young jay thrushes to separate accommodation, because of the aggressive nature of the adult birds – otherwise, they may attack their offspring.

Above: **Black-headed Sibia**
Pairs are more likely to nest when

housed in a well-planted aviary.
Colourful and relatively hardy.

Black-headed Sibia

Heterophasia capistrata
● **Distribution:** India and the surrounding Himalayan region.
● **Size:** 23cm (9in).
● **Diet:** Softbill food, fruit and insects.
● **Sexing:** No visual distinction possible between the sexes.
● **Compatibility:** Generally not troublesome, but at times may prove aggressive.

The attractive Black-headed Sibia is not a difficult species to maintain, but breeding successes are uncommon, possibly because of the difficulty in identifying pairs. They build a cup-shaped nest, using pine needles if these are available, often locating it quite high up in vegetation growing in the aviary. Four eggs form the usual clutch. Hatching occurs after 14 days and, if adequate supplies of livefood are given, the young sibias will leave the nest after a similar interval. Although not talented songsters, these birds have quite attractive calls.

Silver-eared Mesia

Leiothrix argentauris
● **Distribution:** Himalayan region, Southeast Asia and Sumatra.
● **Size:** 18cm (7in).
● **Diet:** Softbill food, fruit, livefood and even small seeds.
● **Sexing:** Hens have greenish rumps.
● **Compatibility:** Quite social.

This species is another member of the large and diverse babbler family, named from the cries they utter when they are on the move. They are easy to cater for in aviary surroundings and can prove hardy in mild areas, since they are often found in high altitudes. The inclusion of a clump of bamboo in their flight can encourage breeding activity; as with other Asian softbills, they use such plants as nesting sites in the wild. Mesias may choose to build their nests quite low down, near the aviary floor. Incubation is shared by both parents until the chicks hatch after 14 days. The chicks should emerge from the nest after a similar period.

Pekin Robin

Leiothrix lutea

● **Distribution:** Himalayas, Southeast Asia extending to China.
● **Size:** 15cm (6in).
● **Diet:** Softbill food, diced fruit and livefood.
● **Sexing:** No reliable distinction exists, although various plumage differences have been suggested.
● **Compatibility:** Best kept in pairs on their own. Known to be inveterate egg stealers from the nests of other birds.

Below: **Pekin Robin**
A popular species, which is easy to keep, and may even take some seed in its diet. Difficult to sex.

Above: **Silver-eared Mesia**
About nine different subspecies are recognized, so individual birds may show slight differences in plumage. It is quite easy to identify pairs, and these may nest. The birds have an attractive song.

For many softbill enthusiasts, the Pekin Robin has provided the introduction to this fascinating group of birds. Despite its name, it is neither a robin, nor confined to China, but is a close relative of the Silver-eared Mesia.

Pekin Robins are colourful and both sexes have an attractive song. They can prove reasonably hardy once acclimatized, but will benefit from the extra feeding period ensured by the provision of artificial lighting in their quarters during the winter. This will also attract them into the shelter; otherwise they can be rather stubborn about roosting under cover. They will take a budgerigar seed mixture in addition to the usual range of softbill foods.

Breeding details are as for the preceding species. The chicks may appear rather large on fledging, but this is quite normal, and surplus weight is soon lost as the birds start to fend for themselves. They moult for the first time at around 12 weeks of age.

Common Shama

Copsychus malabaricus
● **Distribution:** Indian subcontinent, across Southeast Asia to Indonesia.
● **Size:** 28cm (11in).
● **Diet:** Typical softbill diet, with daily offerings of livefood.
● **Sexing:** Hens are smaller, with noticeably shorter tails and duller plumage overall.
● **Compatibility:** Can be mixed with softbills of similar size, but pairs should be kept on their own for breeding purposes.

The pure melodic song of the cock Shama ranks among the most attractive in the whole of the bird kingdom. These are birds of the forest, and should be provided with a well-planted aviary. They are certainly not suitable for caging on a regular basis, since their long tails are easily damaged. The tail is highly mobile and is often flicked back and forth to reveal the Shama's snow-white rump.

Shamas are highly insectivorous and may well come to feed from the hand in time. Like other thrushes, they tend to lead solitary lives in the wild, and in close confinement a pair may squabble outside the breeding period. Shamas will use a nestbox when breeding, building a nest in which up to five eggs are laid. The eggs hatch after about 13 days, and the young birds are likely to fledge when about 17 days old.

Above: **Common Shama**
The beautiful song of the cock bird and attractive coloration of this species have ensured its popular appeal. Shamas are lively and do well in a planted aviary. Pairs housed on their own may breed.

Black-chinned Yuhina

Yuhina nigrimentum
● **Distribution:** From the Himalayas to China.
● **Size:** 10cm (4in).
● **Diet:** Softbill food, a nectar solution, diced fruit and small insects.
● **Sexing:** Hens tend not to sing and have smaller crests.
● **Compatibility:** Aggressive towards each other. Pairs should be housed individually or with unrelated birds of similar size.

Nine species of Yuhina are recognized, of which the Black-chinned is generally the most common. They are very active little birds and frequently use their crests for display. Although they can be kept in flight cages, they are much more likely to breed in a planted aviary. The cup-shaped nest, built of coconut fibres, is usually concealed among vegetation. The clutch of three or four eggs is incubated primarily by the hen, and should start hatching after 12 days. You must provide an ample supply of small insects if the chicks are to be reared. They fledge when nearly two weeks old.

Among the other species sometimes available, the Yellow-naped Yuhina (*Y. flavicollis*) is most frequently advertised. Yuhinas are not entirely hardy, even when acclimatized, and must have additional light for feeding purposes during the winter months in temperate areas.

Above: **Yellow-naped Yuhina**
Unfortunately, these delightful little softbills are difficult to sex. Hens may have smaller crests.

Below: **Black-chinned Yuhina**
These birds can be kept in pairs alongside other small softbills. Also known as flowerpeckers.

Blue-winged Siva

Minla cyanouroptera
● **Distribution:** Himalayas, extending into Southeast Asia.
● **Size:** 15cm (6in).
● **Diet:** Softbill food, diced fruit, small insects and nectar, especially when first obtained.
● **Sexing:** No visual distinction possible between the sexes.
● **Compatibility:** Can be aggressive, especially when breeding.

The Blue-winged Siva is related to the Pekin Robin (see page 93) and needs similar care, although it may prove more delicate when first obtained. Its song is quiet yet melodious. It will settle well in a planted aviary, where it will delight in seeking out insects. Once acclimatized, sivas have been housed outside throughout the year in mild areas, but they will need heating and lighting if acclimatization takes place during the colder months.

If you have obtained a true pair – which is not easy to ascertain – they may attempt to breed. Birds of opposite sexes may show aggression towards each other, and cocks especially will attempt to harass the chicks after fledging. Therefore, move fledglings to separate quarters. Breeding details as for the Pekin Robin.

Below: **Blue-winged Siva**
This species is more subtly coloured than the Pekin Robin, to which it is related. Identifying pairs for breeding is difficult.

Grey-headed Parrotbill

Paradoxornis gularis
● **Distribution:** Himalayas,
extending eastwards into China.
● **Size:** 18cm (7in).
● **Diet:** Softbill food, diced fruit,
insects and small seeds.
● **Sexing:** No visual distinction
possible between the sexes.
● **Compatibility:** Can be kept
together as a group.

Parrotbills are characterized by
their solid beaks, which give them
their common name. They are
members of the babbler family.
The Grey-headed Parrotbill – one
of the larger birds in the group –
has become increasingly common
in aviculture during recent years.

Above: **Grey-headed Parrotbill**
*Parrotbills as a group are not
common in aviculture. Yet they are
not difficult to maintain and will
take some seed in their diet.*

Even so, relatively little is known
about these birds. Parrotbills
resemble tits in their somewhat
jerky movements. They can prove
reasonably hardy, and will certainly
damage sensitive vegetation with
their sturdy beaks.
  In the wild, they usually nest in
shrubs or young trees. Up to four
eggs form the clutch. Incubation
and fledging times are both about
12 days, and it is very important to
provide livefood when there are
chicks in the nest.

STARLINGS
The starlings (Sturnidae) are one of the most widely distributed avian families, with representative species found on all inhabited continents. Various common names are used to describe the 111 species, notably 'starling', 'grackle' and 'mynah'. In aviaries, most starlings are easy to cater for and prove quite hardy.

Pagoda Mynah
Sturnus pagodarum
● **Distribution:** Eastern Afghanistan, Nepal India and Sri Lanka.
● **Size:** 20cm (8in).
● **Diet:** Softbill food plus diced fruit and livefood.
● **Sexing:** Hens may be slightly duller and smaller overall.
● **Compatibility:** Can be housed in small groups or with robust softbills of similar size. For breeding purposes, pairs are best housed individually.

These attractive members of the starling family are easy to keep in aviary surroundings and they can become quite tame. Provide these mynahs with a cockatiel-type nestbox for breeding purposes and they will build a rough nest inside using twigs and other items collected from around their flight. Their eggs are bluish in colour, and four to six eggs form the usual clutch. Incubation lasts for 14 days, and the young mynahs should emerge from the nestbox about 25 days later. At this stage – and certainly once they are eating independently – you can bring them into the home as pets. Pagoda Mynahs are reasonable mimics and will become very confiding when obtained at this early stage.

Hill Mynah
Gracula religiosa
● **Distribution:** Ranges from India across Southeast Asia, including offshore islands.
● **Size:** 30cm (12in).
● **Diet:** Softbill food, mynah pellets, diced fruit and livefood.
● **Sexing:** No visual distinction possible between the sexes.
● **Compatibility:** Can be housed in a group, but pairs are best kept individually.

The Hill Mynah is highly valued as a talking pet, since its powers of mimicry are unrivalled and its intonation is extremely clear. Hill Mynahs are rarely shy, compared with parrots, and will talk freely, even in front of strangers. If you want a Hill Mynah as a companion, be sure to obtain a young bird – known as a 'gaper' because of its habit of begging open beaked for food. Young birds can be distinguished by the relative absence of the fleshy folds of skin, known as wattles, on the back of the head. Adult birds are usually available at a lower price than gapers, because there is often less demand for them.

Below: **Pagoda Mynah**
This attractive species is also known as the Pagoda Starling. Other starlings are often available, but their coloration tends to be more muted. All need similar care.

Above: **Hill Mynah**
*A softbill highly valued as a pet,
but it is also an attractive aviary
occupant. Surgical sexing will be
needed to define a breeding pair.*

When you are teaching a Hill
Mynah to use its powers of
mimicry, repeat the phrase or
sound that you wish it to learn as
many times as possible throughout
the day. Within a relatively short
time, the bird should attempt to
repeat the sound. It is a good idea
to include your address in the
bird's repertoire, so that you can
be traced easily if the mynah
escapes from your home.
However, you can minimize this
risk by making sure that windows
and doors are closed whenever
you open the cage.

Even when housed in the
company of other Hill Mynahs,
these birds will continue repeating
human speech. Indeed, breeding
pairs made up of talking
individuals are not uncommon, and
an increasing number of
aviculturists are now attempting to
breed Hill Mynahs.

Surgical sexing will enable a pair
to be identified with certainty, and
the birds should then be given a
nestbox. Clutch size is usually two
or three eggs, with the incubation
period extending for 15 days.
Some Hill Mynahs may be
reluctant to sit, leaving the nest at
any hint of disturbance, so try to
avoid this. Once the chicks hatch,
provide a good supply of livefood.
Cock birds can become quite
aggressive in defence of the nest
and may attempt to attack their
keeper, so you should exercise a
degree of caution when entering
their aviary. The chicks will
normally leave the nest when they
are about one month old.

Purple Glossy Starling

Lamprotornis purpureus
● **Distribution:** Occurs across a broad band of north Africa, from the Sudan to Senegal, south of the Sahara.
● **Size:** 23cm (9in).
● **Diet:** Softbill food, mynah pellets, fruit and livefood.
● **Sexing:** No visual distinction possible between the sexes.
● **Compatibility:** Can be kept with softbills of similar size, but house pairs in separate accommodation.

Iridescence, a common feature of the plumage of many starlings, is particularly noticeable in this attractive species. They are very active birds that should be kept in a large flight and not caged on a regular basis. Like related species, they are liable to destroy all but the most robust plants if they are kept in a planted aviary. Glossy Starlings delight in bathing, which helps to keep their plumage in top condition.

Apart from the Purple species, another related form, which occurs further south in Africa, is the Green Glossy Starling (*L. chalybeus*),

sometimes also known as the Blue-eared. Long-tailed Glossy Starlings are also seen on occasion, with iridescence present in their plumage.

The birds need a nestbox for breeding purposes and two or three eggs will hatch after 14 days. The young birds will leave the nest at about 21 days and will be independent within a further week. At this point they should be removed from the aviary, to enable the adult birds to nest again and raise a new batch of chicks.

Spreo Starling

Spreo superbus
● **Distribution:** Eastern parts of Africa.
● **Size:** 20cm (8in).
● **Diet:** Softbill food, including mynah pellets, plus fruit and insects.
● **Sexing:** No reliable visual distinction possible; hens may be duller and smaller.
● **Compatibility:** Pairs are best kept on their own, although they tend to be less quarrelsome than other starlings. Two pairs may live together in a large aviary.

Above: **Spreo Starling**
Another African species. It is easy to maintain and often nests quite readily in aviary surroundings.

Sometimes described as the Superb Starling, the Spreo is another quite hardy species, once properly acclimatized in its quarters. Pairs tend to nest readily; indeed, starlings rank among the easiest softbills to breed successfully under aviary conditions. This is partly because larger livefood, such as easily available crickets and mealworms, can be safely fed immediately the chicks have hatched.

Hartlaub's Touraco

Tauraco hartlaubi
● **Distribution:** Eastern Africa.
● **Size:** 40cm (16in).
● **Diet:** Diced fruit, sprinkled with softbill food, mynah pellets, livefood and even chopped greenstuff, such as spinach beet, dandelion leaves and chickweed.
● **Sexing:** No visual distinction possible between the sexes.
● **Compatibility:** Can be housed with other, larger softbills.

Left: **Purple Glossy Starling**
Only in sunlight can you fully appreciate the iridescent sheen on the plumage of these starlings.

Hartlaub's Touraco is one of the more commonly available species. Touracos are unusual birds in several respects. The brilliant red coloration in their flight feathers arises from a unique pigment which, when exposed to alkaline water, may be leached out of the plumage. They can have a zygodactyl perching grip, with two toes directed behind the perch and two positioned in front. Their outer tow can also be moved forward like that of an owl.

Check the birds' toes carefully before buying, since touracos can be susceptible to bumblefoot. They may also suffer from frostbite if they roost outside during bitterly cold weather. However, they are quite hardy once established in their quarters, and with the provision of perch heaters you should be able to keep them out of doors throughout the year.

Below: **Hartlaub's Touraco**
The touracos – a striking group of large softbills – need relatively spacious surroundings. Cocks may turn savage towards their mates at the start of the breeding period.

Grey Go-away Bird

Crinifer concolor
● **Distribution:** East and southern Africa
● **Size:** 50cm (20in).
● **Diet:** Diced fruit, with softbill food, mynah pellets and chopped greenstuff. Will also take livefood.
● **Sexing:** No visual distinction possible between the sexes.
● **Compatibility:** Tend to be aggressive, especially when breeding.

The Go-away Birds, named after the sound of their calls, also belong to the touraco family, Musophagidae. They have very similar habits to their more colourful relatives. When provided with fresh perches, these touracos will eagerly eat any leaves and buds, so they are not really suitable for a small planted aviary. They are also very lively and show to best effect in spacious surroundings.

Their nest, consisting mainly of twigs, is usually built on a suitable

Above: **Grey Go-away Bird**
Another member of the touraco family, but relatively dull in colour. Five predominantly grey species are recognized; some are described as plantain-eaters (a wild banana plant), but show no preference for bananas in captivity. Hens may sometimes be distinguished by their greenish beaks; otherwise, surgical sexing may be needed to identify a pair.

platform. Try to screen this if you can, since touracos can be reluctant to nest in the open. Ensure also that the hen bird is not persecuted by her potential mate. In some cases, you may have to separate the birds for a brief period. The usual clutch consists of two or three eggs, laid on alternate days. Both parents share incubation duties and the chicks should start to hatch after 28 days. They may leave the nest when only three weeks old, although it will be several weeks more before they are able to feed independently.

Red-billed Magpie

Urocissa erythrorhyncha

● **Distribution:** From the Himalayas across Southeast Asia into China.

● **Size:** 60cm (24in).

● **Diet:** Mynah pellets, diced fruit, livefood and similar items.

● **Sexing:** No reliable distinction possible between the sexes. It seems certain that differences in eye coloration are not significant in this respect.

● **Compatibility:** Best kept apart in pairs. Never with smaller birds.

These magnificent corvids need a suitably spacious aviary, where their lively natures will have free expression. They are relatively easy birds to cater for and are quite hardy. Various subspecies are recognized throughout their extensive range and this accounts for slight variations in appearance, which may initially be mistaken for sexual distinctions. The Red-billed Magpie is sometimes described as the Occipital Blue Pie, not to be confused with the Yellow-billed Blue Pie (*Urocissa flavirostris*) which, as its name suggests, has a yellow rather than a red bill.

Three to six eggs form the usual clutch, and these should hatch after a period of 17 days. Avoid disturbances at this stage, and provide a high level of animal protein in the diet while the chicks are being reared. They will fledge about three weeks after hatching.

Below: **Red-billed Magpie**
One of the most spectacular softbills. Although they are easy to keep, these members of the crow family need a large aviary. House pairs on their own; they can prove highly aggressive, even towards each other, and may suddenly turn on other birds sharing their accommodation. Surgical sexing is the only reliable means of sexing individuals of this species. Avoid disturbances during the nesting period and remove the youngsters once they are feeding themselves, as the adults may attack them.

White-tailed Jay

Cyanocorax mystacalis

● **Distribution:** Arid areas of southwestern Ecuador, extending into northwestern Peru.
● **Size:** 30cm (12in).
● **Diet:** Omnivorous, requiring fruit and softbill food, plus mynah pellets, livefood and similar foodstuffs.
● **Sexing:** No visual distinction possible between the sexes.
● **Compatibility:** Pairs can be aggressive, so do not house them with smaller birds.

Various species of jay are occasionally available. These birds make attractive aviary occupants, since they will become quite tame in captivity and possess highly inquisitive natures.

Pairs frequently attempt to breed, building a nest of twigs and similar material in a shrub. You may be able to persuade them to use a suitably disguised artificial platform, which will provide a more secure base for the nest. Four eggs usually form the clutch. These will hatch in 16 days and the young birds leave the nest about three weeks later.

Above: **White-tailed Jay**
Attractive and lively aviary occupants, these jays usually become quite tame and may nest successfully in captivity.

Below: **Inca Jay**
Like other members of the crow family, jays are hardy once they have become fully acclimatized.

African Paradise Flycatcher

Tersiphone viridis

● **Distribution:** Africa, south of the Sahara.
● **Size:** Can be very variable, depending on tail length. At least 30cm (12in), overall.
● **Diet:** Livefood, softbill food and mynah pellets.
● **Sexing:** Hens have much shorter tails than cocks, and no white plumage.
● **Compatibility:** Pairs are best kept apart from other birds.

The African Paradise Flycatcher is a most striking species. The spectacular appearance of the adult cock is not achieved until it is at least three years old. Until that age, it resembles the adult hen.

The birds build a cup-shaped nest in vegetation. Both sexes share the incubation and rearing duties, which last approximately 16 days and 14 days respectively. A virtually unlimited supply of livefood is essential for rearing purposes.

Similar flycatchers are also found in Asia, but can prove equally difficult to 'meat off' on to a more inert diet, showing a distinct preference for livefood. For this reason, flycatchers generally are not birds which can be recommended to the novice softbill keeper.

Below: **Paradise Flycatcher**
A cock bird feeding a brood of chicks. The young will need a constant supply of livefood.

Rufous-bellied Niltava

Niltava sundara

- **Distribution:** From the Himalayas, across Southeast Asia to China.
- **Size:** 18cm (7in).
- **Diet:** Livefood, softbill food and pellets, fruit.
- **Sexing:** Cocks are much more colourful, hens being predominantly brownish with a blue spot on each side of the neck.
- **Compatibility:** Keep pairs apart, although they will live satisfactorily in captivity alongside other softbills of similar size.

Above: **Rufous-bellied Niltava**
This is clearly a cock bird, being much more colourful than the mainly brown female.

These flycatchers can be delicate when first obtained and need to be kept warm, at an ambient temperature of about 18°C (64°F). Once acclimatized, however, they can prove reasonably hardy. They show a natural preference for livefood and require a densely planted flight where they can forage for insects, but do encourage them to eat a variety of other foods. If the birds do not have access to an outside aviary, you will need to provide regular bathing facilities.

Niltavas often favour a ledge or open-fronted nestbox as a nesting site, and will need moss for the nest itself. Four eggs form a typical clutch, and during the incubation period of 14 days the hen sits alone. An unlimited supply of livefood is important to ensure that the chicks are reared satisfactorily. The supply must also be maintained throughout the post-weaning period, woodlice often being favoured by these birds. The chicks will leave the nest when they are about 14 days old.

Below: **Rufous-bellied Niltava**
A hen bird. The hen may lay four eggs and incubates alone. Suitable livefood is vital at this time.

Lesser Green Broadbill

Calyptomena viridis
● **Distribution:** Malay Peninsula, Borneo and Sumatra.
● **Size:** 16.5cm (6.5in).
● **Diet:** Fruit, softbill food, mynah pellets and livefood.
● **Sexing:** Hens are duller overall and also lack the black markings of the cock bird.
● **Compatibility:** Often kept in tropical houses alongside other species.

This particular species of broadbill is generally frugivorous in its feeding habits, making it relatively easy to adapt to aviary life. However, the birds are sensitive to cold and are often kept indoors, with heating if necessary.

Above: **Lesser Green Broadbill**
A spectacular, if somewhat shy, species that thrives best in a planted tropical house setting. It needs warm surroundings and a diet that includes plenty of fruit.

There are 18 recognized species in all, but only the Green Broadbills are usually seen in aviculture. In the wild, they live in dense jungle. Their relatively large eyes seem to suggest that they are crepuscular by nature (i.e. active at dawn and dusk), but very little is known about their habits.

Their nests, commonly located above water, are elaborate structures, suspended from the branch above by strands of nesting material.

Blue-winged Pitta

Pitta moluccensis (brachyura)
● **Distribution:** Across the Indian subcontinent to Indonesia and Japan. (Several forms are recognized through this range and are sometimes classified as separate species, such as *P.brachyura).*
● **Size:** 20cm (8in).
● **Diet:** Livefood plus softbill food, including mynah pellets and fruit.
● **Sexing:** No visual distinction possible between the sexes.
● **Compatibility:** Keep these birds on their own, since they are aggressive towards both pittas and other birds. Supervise them closely when in breeding condition.

Because of their feeding habits and general behaviour, pittas as a group are essentially birds for the

Above: **Blue-winged Pitta**
The ground-dwelling pittas are predominantly insectivorous in their feeding habits. They are highly aggressive and need specialist care and supervision.

specialist. They are normally highly insectivorous, and it is difficult to persuade them to take inanimate food. Pittas are ground-dwelling species, although they may roost at night on a convenient perch. The floor covering of their quarters is important if the birds are not to succumb to foot ailments; peat is preferable, but it must be kept moist to prevent it from becoming dusty. It is likely that this species lays a clutch of up to five eggs. Hatching begins after 18 days and the chicks leave the nest after a similar period.

Grey-headed Kingfisher

Halcyon leucocephala
● **Distribution:** From the Cape Verde Islands across equatorial Africa eastwards to Yemen.
● **Size:** 20cm (8in).
● **Diet:** Livefood and similar items, softbill food and mynah pellets.
● **Sexing:** No visual distinction possible between the sexes.
● **Compatibility:** Can be kept together in small groups.

Kingfishers as a family are not common avicultural subjects, but some – notably those native to either arid or forested areas – are relatively easy to maintain in aviary surroundings. The Grey-headed Kingfisher among others, has been bred in captivity. Rather than use a nestbox, the birds excavate a nest in the side of a specially constructed walled area in the aviary. The bank needs to be firm, so that it does not collapse on the birds as they tunnel inwards. You should therefore incorporate a false nesting hole, using a drainage tube to provide access, with a chamber behind. The access should extend back for 25cm (10in) or so. If they are deprived of the opportunity to tunnel, the beaks of these kingfishers tend to become overgrown.

Kingfishers are essentially insectivorous, consuming a variety of livefood. They will take other items, including some fish, as part of their diet, with whitebait being a favoured rearing food for chicks. Incubation, shared by both parents, lasts 18 days and the young kingfishers emerge from the nesting tunnel after a similar period. Take particular care when providing water for these birds: if they have not had access to bathing facilities for some time, they may drown.

Below: **Grey-headed Kingfisher**
Not all kingfishers feed on fish; forest and dry country species are insectivorous and easy to keep.

White-breasted Water Rail

Laterallus leucopyrrhus
● **Distribution:** Southeastern South America, from Brazil to Uruguay and Paraguay.
● **Size:** 18cm (7in).
● **Diet:** Softbill food, including mynah pellets, livefood and small seeds.
● **Sexing:** No visual distinction possible between the sexes.
● **Compatibility:** Best kept apart from other ground-dwelling species in aviary conditions.

White-breasted Water Rails are largely terrestrial in their habits, but will fly if disturbed. Catching them in aviary surroundings can be difficult, for they are exceptionally nimble.

They need an aviary which includes a small pond and low vegetation because they tend to be rather nervous and will dart into cover if they feel threatened.

These interesting but rather secretive birds can be kept out of doors quite safely during the summer months. However, they

need protection against frostbite in cold weather and are best transferred to indoor accommodation at such times.

They build a woven, cup-shaped nest, in which they lay a clutch of four or five eggs. On hatching, about 25 days later, the young birds start foraging for food with their parents. They will relish finely chopped hard-boiled egg and small insects at this stage. The youngsters can be left safely with the adults since they are unlikely to molest them.

Below: **White-breasted Water Rail**
Rails are not particularly common avicultural subjects, but this species is quite regularly available, and has been bred a number of times. These rather nervous birds need the cover of a densely planted flight and an area of shallow water. They will remain hidden for much of the time, venturing forth to feed. They do occasionally perch, but are unlikely to disturb other birds in their quarters; nor are rails aggressive towards each other.

Lilac-breasted Roller
Coracias cuadata
- **Distribution:** Southern parts of Africa, below the equator.
- **Size:** 30cm (12in).
- **Diet:** Livefood and similar items, softbill food and mynah pellets.
- **Sexing:** No visual distinction possible between the sexes.
- **Compatibility:** May tend to prove aggressive.

This species is similar in appearance to the Indian Blue Roller (*C. benghalensis*), but can be easily distinguished by its strongly forked tail. The birds are named after their pattern of flight, since they will catch flying insects on the wing, hawking them out of the air. They will also dart down to seize insects and small creatures on the ground, including young mice and lizards. They are, however, largely insectivorous, and cockroaches and locusts are popular foods for rollers.

These birds have bred in aviary surroundings, using a nestbox. They may lay up to five eggs, which are incubated for 18 days by both parents. Fledging normally occurs by the time the chicks are four weeks old.

Below: **Lilac-breasted Roller**
An insectivorous species that can prove difficult to 'meat off' on to a largely inanimate diet. Provide food supplements on livefood.

Cedar Waxwing

Bombycilla cedrorum

- **Distribution:** North America, moving southwards during the winter to the Caribbean and South America.
- **Size:** 18cm (7in).
- **Diet:** Softbill food, fruit, especially raisins and pyracantha berries. May even eat greenfood. Will take increasing quantities of livefood when chicks are being reared.
- **Sexing:** No visual distinction possible between the sexes
- **Compatibility:** Tends not to be aggressive towards birds of similar size in captivity.

As might be expected from their wide distribution, waxwings are hardy birds and can be kept in an

Above: **Cedar Waxwing**
An attractive species, named after the reddish wing markings that resemble droplets of sealing wax.

outdoor aviary throughout the year. A group of these attractive softbills can be housed together. They will build their nests at various sites in a planted aviary. The clutch consists of two or three eggs, with an incubation period of 14 days. During the summer, as soon as the young hatch, the adult birds become much more active, chasing and catching flies and midges which they feed to the chicks. Of course, you should supply additional livefood at this time. Fledging usually occurs when the young waxwings are about three weeks old.

Index to species

Page numbers in **bold** indicate major references, including accompanying photographs. Page numbers in *italics* indicate captions to other illustrations. Less important text entries are shown in normal type.

Further reading

Alderton, D. *Looking after Cage Birds* Ward Lock, 1982
Alderton, D. *The Complete Cage and Aviary Bird Handbook* Pelham Books, 1986
Arnall, L. and Keymer, I.F. *Bird Diseases* Balliere Tindall, 1975
Goodwin, D. *Crows of the World* British Museum (Natural History), 1976
Harper, D. *Pet Birds for Home and Garden* Salamander Books Ltd., 1986
Mobbs, A.J. *Hummingbirds* Triplegate, 1982
Roots, C. *Softbilled Birds* John Gifford, 1970
Rutgers, A. *The Handbook of Foreign Birds* Volume I Blandford Press, 1964
Rutgers, A. and Norris, K.A. (Editors) *Encyclopaedia of Aviculture* Volumes I to III Blandford Press, 1977
Snow, D.W. *The Cotingas* British Museum (Natural History), 1982
Vince, C. *Keeping Softbilled Birds* Stanley Paul, 1980

In addition, various field guides contain information concerning the identification and behaviour of softbills in the wild.

Picture credits

Artists
Copyright of the artwork illustrations on the pages following the artists' names is the property of Salamander Books Ltd.

Guy Troughton: 30-1, 58

Brian Watson (Linden Artists): 23

Peter Young: 55(T)

Photographs
Unless otherwise stated, all the photographs have been taken by and are the copyright of Cyril Laubscher. The publishers wish to thank the following photographers who have supplied other photographs for this book. The photographs have been credited by page number and position on the page: (B)Bottom, (T)Top, (C)Centre, (BL)Bottom left etc.

Ideas into Print: 42(B), 43

Eliot Lyons: 83

Acknowledgements
The publishers wish to thank the following for their help in preparing this book: Chris Allaway; Eric and Sylvia Allaway; Paul and June Bailey; Bob Beeson; Harry Bishop; Blean Bird Park; Dave and Rose Coles; Mick and Marian Cripps; Julian Faulkner; Ray and Kathleen Fisk; Jeff Foreman; Brian Gibbs; Rodney and Joan Hamilton; Jeff Hayes; Phil Holland; Ron James; Tim Kemp; Errol Laubscher; Denis and Doreen Lewis; Roy and Diane Lloyd-Roberts; Oaklands Park Farm Aviaries; Arthur and Gwen O'Bray; Ron Oxley; Mike and Jane Pickering; Mick and Beryl Plose; Harry Porter; Porters Fanciers Store; Alan and Janet Ralph; Judy Raven; Ron Rayner; Dave Russell; Raymond Sawyer; Charlie Smith; Tony Smith; Maurice Scholier; Nigel Taboney; Peter Walker; Rosemary Wiseman, Cliff Wright; Tony and Jean Youe. Rita Hemsley (for typing the author's manuscript); Amanda Harrison for editorial assistance.

Blue-winged Pitta